*f*P

# UNDER PRESSURE

*The Final Voyage of Submarine* S-Five

# A. J. Hill

THE FREE PRESS

New York • London • Toronto • Sydney • Singapore

THE FREE PRESS
A Division of Simon & Schuster, Inc.
1230 Avenue of the Americas
New York, NY 10020

For information regarding special discounts for bulk purchases,
please contact Simon & Schuster Special Sales:
1-800-456-6798 or business@simonandschuster.com

Designed by Katy Riegel

Manufactured in the United States of America

1   3   5   7   9   10   8   6   4   2

Library of Congress Cataloging-in-Publication Data
Hill, A. J. (Alvin Joseph)
Under pressure : the final voyage of Submarine S-5 / A. J. Hill.
p.   cm.
Includes index.
1. S-5 (Submarine)   2. Cooke, Charles Maynard.   3. Submarine disasters—
United States.   4. Search and rescue operations—Atlantic Ocean.   I. Title.
VA65.S15 H54   2002
910'.9163'46—dc21                                   2002071271

ISBN 0-7432-3677-7

The photograph of Midshipman Cooke (Figure 1) appears courtesy
of Maynard Horiuchi.
The following photographs appear courtesy of the Naval Historical Foundation,
Washington, D.C.: Figure 2, Figure 12, and Figure 13.
The schematic of the S-Five (Figure 3) was created by the author.
All remaining photographs appear courtesy of the National Archives
at College Park, Maryland.

*This book is dedicated to my wife, Marcy;*
*my daughter, Christie; and*
*my son, Aaron.*

# Contents

# UNDER
# PRESSURE

# Prologue

"Eternal father strong to save
Whose arm hath bound the restless wave,
Who bidd'st the mighty ocean deep
Its own appointed limits keep,
O' hear us when we cry to Thee
For those in peril on the sea."

—WILLIAM WHITING

SEPTEMBER 1, 1920, 13:30—
LAT. 38.30 N, LON. 74.03 W.

Fifty miles off the coast of New Jersey, United States Submarine *S-Five* cruised southwestward, forging steadily through white-capped seas that broke against her starboard side and rolled across her low wooden deck. On the open bridge atop her conning tower Lt. Commander Charles "Savvy" Cooke steadied himself against the forward gunwale, lifted his binoculars and scanned the horizon. The powerful glasses showed only empty ocean and long green swells sweeping out of the north.

It was a fine late summer day, clear and bright with a hint of fall in the air. Slanting down between high scattered clouds, sunlight sparkled from the waves and made rainbows in the spray over the *S-Five*'s foredeck. Savvy had sent the lookout below, so he had the bridge to himself. As he gazed out across the wide Atlantic, with the wind in his hair and the sunlight warming his shoulders, he felt happier than he had in a long time. The war against Germany was now more than a year in the past, but it had created lasting domestic problems in the United States. Instead of a hero's welcome, many returning servicemen had found only inflation and rampant unemployment; but these hardships hadn't affected Savvy. Instead, the war's end had released him from a long and unwelcome tour of shore duty. Back at sea now and in command of his own boat, he was content or almost so.

It had been nearly a year since he'd last seen his children. He could still picture them on the day he'd said goodbye, standing beside their grandmother in the doorway of the little farmhouse in Arkansas and looking up at him with their mother's wide blue eyes. Anne, the younger one, had clung to him tearfully, her usually cheerful face twisted with sorrow, but Temple had held back, staring up at him in silent reproach. She'd been only a year old when her mother died, too young to understand the tragedy, but old enough sense the loss. Her look haunted Savvy now, as he stood on the S-Five's bridge watching waves march across the sea.

A high-pitched whistle pierced his reverie. Pulling himself back to the present, he looked down through the open hatchway into the steering compartment that formed the bulk of the conning tower.

"Yes, helmsman?"

"Control room calling, Sir," the helmsman responded. "Mr. Grisham reports speed run complete, hatches secure, and vents closed. All stations manned and ready."

Lieutenant Grisham was the sub's executive officer. Savvy had been waiting for his report. Lifting the binoculars again, he checked the sea one last time. Nothing had changed. No sails were visible, no smoke trails marred the clean arc of the horizon. Stowing the glasses in their watertight case below the gunwale, he removed a stopwatch from the pocket of his windbreaker and carefully set the hands to zero. Then he bent down to the hatch, raised his voice over the noise of wind and waves, and shouted, "Dive! Dive!" At the same moment he triggered the stopwatch and shoved it back into his pocket. The time was 1:53.

A klaxon began blaring inside the sub. Savvy stooped, grabbed the hatch rim, and in one fluid motion swung himself down through it. The hatch cover jerked back and forth several times, then slammed shut. Moments later waves began breaking over the conning tower as the *S-Five* slipped below the surface. Within less than a minute after Savvy's order the submarine had vanished, slanting silently down into the cool green depths at a speed of more than ten knots.

Two and a half minutes later, still traveling at high speed, the *S-Five* plowed into the sea floor 180 feet below. Rebounding through a cloud of sand and silt, she struck again, and this time buried her nose in the bottom. Her propellers spun to a halt. The water around her cleared. From various places along her hull, lines of bubbles and thin streamers of oil wavered up toward the distant surface. Otherwise, nothing moved.

# 1

# THE BEGINNING

"I saw the new moon late yestreen
Wi' the auld moon in her arm;
And if we gang to sea, master,
I fear we'll come to harm."

— TRADITIONAL BALLAD

MONDAY, AUGUST 30, 1920, 12:00—
BOSTON NAVY YARD.

At noon on Monday, August 30, United States Submarine *S-Five* edged away from her berth at the old Boston Navy Yard in Charlestown and with her engines barely idling glided down the Mystic River into Boston's Outer Harbor. By mid-afternoon she had passed the high granite tower of the Minot's Ledge Lighthouse and headed out to sea. As soon as she was clear of land, her commanding officer ordered a dive to "trim up" or balance the sub. This was required at the beginning of every cruise in order to compensate for any changes in weight since the sub's last time out.

It was an exciting day for the forty officers and enlisted men on board the *S-Five;* after a summer filled with training exercises they were finally setting out on their first genuine mission. According to the itinerary that they had received with their orders in August, they would spend the next four weeks traveling from port to port as part of a Navy campaign to attract "ex-servicemen" to its growing submarine fleet. By Friday, September 3, they were scheduled to arrive in Baltimore, Maryland. After spending five days on display there, they'd continue down the east coast with similar stops in Washington, Richmond, and Savannah before rejoining their flotilla in Boston at the end of September.

During peacetime, a high-profile recruiting mission like this was a prestigious beginning for a new submarine. For Savvy Cooke and his crew it was also a welcome relief from the six long months they had spent making the *S-Five* ready for sea: months filled with the seemingly endless routines of testing, retesting, and, when necessary, repairing every machine, circuit, valve, and joint in one of the most complex naval vessels afloat.

The new assignment hadn't spared them from the Navy's red tape. Twice each year the service's Bureau of Steam Engineering required a series of performance evaluations from every ship on active duty. On August 20 Savvy had received orders to complete the Bureau's current testing program during the voyage to Baltimore.

The evaluation consisted of four parts. First were two endurance tests: a twenty-four-hour surface run followed by a five-hour submerged run. Then came a pair of high speed runs: four hours on the surface and one hour submerged. Altogether these four tests were designed to probe the sub's power plant during every combination of high and low speed, on the surface and beneath it.

For a newly commissioned submarine such exercises should be little more than a formality; the *S-Five* had undergone far more rigorous testing during her recent sea trials. The same went for her crew. After the summer of intensive training that Savvy had put them through, the *S-Five*'s men should find nothing challenging in the tests. With one possible exception.

The potential ringer was the crash dive that was required before the final underwater sprint. Normally employed only during wartime, crash dives had a single primary goal: to get submarines underwater as quickly as possible. By Navy criteria that meant *very* quickly. According to its *Rules for Engineering Performance,* a competent submarine crew should be able to take their vessel to periscope depth—about forty feet—in under a minute. Sixty seconds was not much time in which to convert an entire 800-ton sub from surface to submerged configuration *and* get her safely to a depth of forty feet; but it was certainly possible. Savvy understood that crack German crews had been able to do it in under *thirty* seconds.

Since beginning sea trials in May the crew of the *S-Five* had performed forty dives, fifteen of which had been crashes. Ordinarily this should have been sufficient schooling, but the Navy's rules also required training dives to be performed by the members of a single watch. As a result, each of the *S-Five's* three watch sections had performed only half a dozen crash dives. This wasn't enough practice for so demanding a maneuver and it showed in their results. The best time for a crash dive by any section had been two minutes and fourteen seconds, a far cry from the Bureau's one-minute standard. The impending dive would give the third watch an opportunity to improve their record, but Savvy didn't expect them to achieve one minute.

As soon as the boat had been trimmed outside Boston Harbor, Savvy had her brought back to the surface. At two o'clock on Monday afternoon she began the twenty-four-hour endurance run. For the rest of the day she maintained a steady twelve knots almost due east. In the evening, while the sun turned the western horizon scarlet, she rounded Cape Cod, put up her running lights, and started south toward Nantucket.

Hour after hour the tireless diesels drove the sub through the night, while the watches came and went and the engineers ran through their checklists, recording data from the testing. Well after dark, with the Nantucket Shoals Lightship hard on her starboard beam, the *S-Five* turned again, this time toward the southwest for the 450-mile run to the mouth of the Chesapeake Bay. Dawn found her well out of sight of land, still cruising at twelve knots, on a heading of 220 degrees. The first endurance test still had eight hours to run.

CHARLES MAYNARD COOKE JUNIOR was a few inches shy of six feet, with a compact, athletic physique that he maintained through regular shipboard workouts with a medicine ball. Beneath an unruly shock of light brown hair, his high forehead and regular features gave him a youthful appearance, but he wasn't handsome; his ears were too large for that and his nose had been broken too many times.

According to a marine guard who once served under him, Cooke was a "no-nonsense type, typical old Navy." Even his daughter admitted that he was never a "hail fellow, well met" kind of person. Yet he was known as an impartial and considerate commanding officer and his crews were keenly loyal to him. Although his serious expression and military bearing seemed to indicate a stiff, humorless personality, closer inspection revealed a hint of laughter lurking in his pale blue eyes. In fact, when he was in relaxed circumstances, it was more than a hint, according to friends who had seen him impersonate a temperance officer disposing of a case of whiskey while sampling each bottle.

Whatever people might have thought of Cooke's personality, no one doubted his intelligence. After completing college in only two years, he had gone on at age nineteen to attend the United States Naval Academy at Annapolis, graduating four years later in second place in his class. At the Academy he'd acquired the nickname "Savvy" that would stick with him throughout his career, replacing the less colorful "Chob" that his family had used when he was a boy. According to his classmates, the moniker reflected Savvy's common sense and practicality as much as his academic brilliance.

In 1920 Savvy had been in the Navy for fourteen years: seven of them in submarines. The *S-Five* was his third command. She'd been built at the Portsmouth Naval Shipyard in Kittery, a small town fifty miles north of Boston that still prides itself in being "The Oldest Incorporated Town in Maine." The Navy Yard was more than a century old when the *S-Five* was launched, although shipbuilding had been going on in the neighboring town of Portsmouth for twice that long, ever since the Royal Navy's HMS *Falkland* was launched there in 1690.

As the eighteenth century drew to a close the United States needed a supply of large frigates in order to compete with the great European navies, notably those of Britain and France. To achieve this end, Congress established the Navy Department in 1798 and appropriated funds for six new warships, but it soon became apparent that the private boatyards of the day lacked sufficient docking and storage space to handle such ambitious projects. So Congress authorized the Navy to set up its own shipbuilding facilities at six sites along the east coast of the United States. The first of the Navy Yards was at Portsmouth—although the group of small islands that comprised it actually belonged to the town of Kittery on the Maine side of the river.

During its first decades the Portsmouth Navy Yard acquired a well-deserved reputation for quality nautical construction. As a result, in 1855 it was given the coveted task of repairing the famous old warship, U.S.S. *Constitution,* otherwise known as "Old Ironsides." Sixty years later, when the Navy decided to build its own submarines instead of buying them from private contractors, it once again chose the Portsmouth yard as its primary site.

WHEN SAVVY ARRIVED in Kittery in late December 1919, the *S-Five* had been under construction for two years. Although she'd been launched a month previously on November 10, she was still little more than a hollow shell with engines. The remainder of her "fitting out" would be Savvy's responsibility.

The young lieutenant commander was well qualified for the assignment. For two years he'd served as assistant inspector of machinery at the Fore River Shipyard, a private Navy contractor in Quincy, Massachusetts. While there he'd overseen the construction of more than twenty submarines, providing fighting ships, as he was fond of saying, for some of the U.S. Navy's most "zealous" submarine captains during World War I.

Savvy was under no illusions about what was at stake in Portsmouth. For two decades the submarine industry had been at the center of a three-way conflict between the Navy Department and two civilian firms: John Holland's Electric Boat Company, located in Massachusetts, and the Lake Torpedo Boat Company in Connecticut. Neither company seemed capable of producing a satisfactory result: among other things, the Electric Boat Company's diesel engines were notorious for vibration and overheating, while Lake's submarines had poor diving qualities.

By 1916 these problems had become intolerable. As the head of the Navy's Submarine Section stated in a memo to the chief of naval operations, the desire of the commercial companies to maximize profits often resulted in submarines that could pass the Navy's performance tests but were neither safe nor efficient fighting machines. As a result, he said, the line officers whose lives depended on these vessels were "in revolt." His opinion was shared by the heads of the Bureau of Construction and Repair (BUC&R) and the Bureau of Steam Engineering (BUENG), who also expressed concern that the Electric Boat Company intended to establish a monopoly in submarine construction, a development that would surely make matters worse.

It was to forestall this possibility that the Navy established its state-of-the-art facility at Portsmouth. By demonstrating how submarines *ought* to be built, the new yard would put pressure on the civilian companies to do a better job, while at the same time providing a source of high quality boats for the Navy. To test this assumption the first three of the new S-Class submarines were distributed among the builders: the *S-One* was assigned to Electric Boat, the *S-Two* went to Lake's company, and the *S-Three* was given to Portsmouth.

Sure enough, the Navy yard completed the *S-Three* in seventeen months, half the time that the private companies required for their subs, and the new boat functioned quite well. The Yard's next project, the *S-Four*, took only twenty-three months; but by December 1919, it had become clear that this boat was seriously flawed. For example her diesels (supplied by the Electric Boat

Company) shook so badly that her maximum operating speed had to be reduced by two and a half knots, and the vibration dampers that were installed to cure the problem merely created another when they became soaked with oil and generated smoke.

It was obvious to Savvy that he was expected to prevent similar problems from occurring with the *S-Five*. He wasted no time living up to his reputation. Within three months, on March 6, the Navy's newest S-Boat was commissioned, the ceremony having been pushed ahead to facilitate early testing. Within five months she was ready to begin sea trials.

As the *S-Five*'s commanding officer and the person in charge of her completion, Savvy was often called upon to guide visiting bigwigs through the boat; and after the commissioning ceremony, it seemed that hardly a week passed—when the sub was in port—that she didn't attract a bunch of well-connected visitors, eager to see firsthand this impressive, and at $1.5 million ($33.5 million in today's dollars), expensive new sub.

Although submarines are extraordinarily complex machines, their *basic* structure is simple: from a distance the *S-Five* resembled a long steel cylinder with a wedge-shaped bow and a pointed stern. Her most salient feature was the streamlined "conning tower" fifteen feet high, twenty feet long, and only six feet wide that rose above her deck, looking so much like a fat sail that modern sailors actually refer to it as "the sail." On its lower level the conning tower consisted of an enclosed "steering platform" from which the helmsman guided the boat both above and below the surface. A ring of four-inch-diameter portholes set at eye level around the steering platform afforded a panoramic view of the outside, except directly astern. Most of the time, however, the helmsman steered by compass headings using directions relayed from the bridge. This was on the conning tower's upper level, a tear-shaped platform enclosed by a broad chest-high bulkhead, from which lookouts could scan the surrounding ocean and the officer of the deck could maneuver the sub.

A flat wooden deck covered the *S-Five*'s rounded pressure hull over most of its length, with a flared area just forward of the conning tower for a deck-gun emplacement. At intervals along the deck large cargo hatches, each more than three feet across, gave access to the sub's interior. There were four of them, one for each internal compartment except the control room, which was covered by the conning tower. Smaller "personnel" hatches provided access through the conning tower. During surface cruising waves commonly swept across the deck, making the cargo hatches unusable during much of the time at sea.

The S-*Five*'s interior reflected the shape of her hull: a long hollow cigar shape fifteen feet in diameter and two hundred feet long. Reinforced partitions, called bulkheads, divided the interior into sections, and horizontal decks split each section lengthwise. The result was a series of five compartments, each about forty feet long, with a curved overhead, a flat deck, and a large bilge space beneath it. The bilges were particularly important, because they acted as sumps, so that water and oil didn't pool on the decks. They were equipped with a drainage system, so that their contents could be pumped overboard periodically.

A watertight door in the center of each bulkhead connected adjacent compartments. These doorways were narrow—eighteen inches across—and only four feet tall, with sills raised a foot off the deck to prevent water in one compartment from running into the next. Occasionally one of the sailors would demonstrate how submariners negotiated the doorways at a dead run, either diving through head first or swinging through feet first without missing a stride. To withstand high pressures, the doors themselves were heavy and mounted on massive hinges. A series of metal levers, called dogs, around the perimeter of each door allowed it to be sealed tightly in the event of an accident.

Compartments were named for their principal functions. From bow to stern these were: torpedo room, battery room, control room, engine room, and motor room. Savvy quickly learned that most people weren't interested in dry technical explanations as they toured these spaces. They preferred instead to hear stories of "human interest," except in the torpedo room, where the sleek, deadly shapes in their great steel cradles seemed to fascinate everyone. The *S-Five* carried twelve torpedoes. Twenty feet long, twenty-one inches in diameter, and weighing more than a ton apiece, these underwater missiles were the sub's main offensive armament. In their detachable warheads each could carry hundreds of pounds of high explosive, enough to cripple or sink any warship afloat.

Nevertheless, Savvy explained, submarines didn't always attack while submerged and didn't always use torpedoes to sink their prey. Torpedoes were expensive and often in short supply. Moreover they weren't the most reliable devices, frequently going off course, running too high or too low, or simply failing to explode. In fact, whenever possible submarine commanders preferred to attack on the surface, using their deck guns to overpower small or lightly armed opponents.

On a more practical level, Savvy described how the crew in the torpedo room used overhead tracks and chain hoists to manhandle their huge charges. Using these tools, he asserted, one man could load and fire a torpedo weighing more than ten times his own weight.

Besides the torpedoes, people seemed to be most impressed by the bunks in the forward compartment.

"Do you mean, men actually *sleep* here?" someone was bound to ask, indicating the thin, metal-framed mattresses chained up against the walls.

"Well, yes," Savvy would answer, adding that most of the crew, including the sub's officers, bunked in the battery room, the next compartment aft.

Compared to the torpedo room there was little to see in the battery room. The batteries themselves were housed beneath the deck, leaving the space above relatively bare, except for personal lockers and the triple tier of bunks along either side. This gave visitors ample opportunity to examine closely packed and uncomfortable-looking berths in detail. It was fun to watch civilians eye the narrow spaces between the suspended mattresses and imagine trying to sleep there; but an even bigger kick came from the expressions of officers from the surface navy when they learned that the Captain's "stateroom" on this showpiece submarine was nothing more than a set of curtains pulled around one of the bunks.

Next came the control room, in every sense the heart of the sub. With its bewildering array of dials, gauges, switches, wheels, and levers, this compartment was more than most people could take in at one time. After a cursory glance over the banks of controls, they usually contented themselves with looking through the periscopes and climbing up the ladder to the conning tower. As they passed single file through the narrow hallway leading aft to the engine room, they could also poke their heads into the undersized portside cubicle containing the sub's compact galley and the equally cramped "radio shack" directly across from it.

Almost everyone had seen diesel engines of one sort or another, but the eight-cylinder monsters extending along both sides of the engine room's central catwalk were on a scale most people had never encountered. The rocker arms alone were longer than a man's arm. Visitors usually spent their time here simply staring.

The most entertaining part of the tour came when guests had packed themselves in among the pumps, compressors, and drive motors in the last compartment, the motor room. The announcement that this was the end of the tour usually prompted someone to point out the additional watertight door located in the after bulkhead, whereupon Savvy would open it with a flourish to reveal the tiller room, which contained the immense gears linking the sub's helm to the rudders. The tiller room was tiny, about the size of a broom closet. While adventurous individuals squeezed one-by-one into this claustrophobic cubbyhole, others could examine with various degrees of fascination or trepidation the nearby crew's "head," or toilet, with its limited elbow room and complex high-pressure flushing mechanism. If there were no women present, Savvy might explain the potential for error here and the indelicate meaning of "getting your own back." If the rumor was true, a submarine had been lost several years earlier when its captain made a catastrophic mistake in flushing the head.

By the time they climbed out through the motor room hatch,

most people were happy to stretch, take a deep breath, and thank their stars they weren't members of the submarine service. If they hadn't understood it before, the tour usually convinced them that submariners were a special breed.

SAVVY TOOK OFFICIAL COMMAND of the *S-Five* during her commissioning ceremony on March 6, 1920, but this was merely another formality. The task of making the new sub ready for sea would continue through the end of the summer. There was equipment to install, repairs and modifications to complete, and a seemingly endless series of tests to carry out. Last of all there were the sea trials, final practical proof that the *S-Five* could perform up to Navy specifications. Beginning in early May in Massachusetts Bay, the trials lasted until mid-August. The *S-Five* did extremely well in them, acquiring a reputation around the Yard for being a "darling" boat. Nevertheless, when she set out for Baltimore on the recruiting drive at the end of August, several problems remained unresolved.

Perhaps the most worrisome problem involved the "main induction system." Designed to distribute fresh air through the sub's interior when she was on the surface, this system collected the air through large intakes high in the conning tower and channeled it into a sixteen-inch pipe that ran along the top of the hull beneath the deck. Branches went to ventilator outlets in every compartment except the battery room, each of which was equipped with an individual shut-off valve. In addition, the entire system could be isolated using a single large valve, the main induction valve, located in the overhead of the control room. This was the source of the trouble: the *S-Five*'s main induction valve was extremely hard to move. According to the sub's executive officer, it was "all one man could do to close it."

Savvy and his engineers had devoted considerable attention to the stubborn valve, but so far they'd been unable to identify or correct the underlying problem. To make matters worse, during the summer Savvy learned that his sub wasn't the only one to have this trouble. In late spring the skipper of the *S-Five*'s sister ship, the *S-Four*, returned from a training cruise along the east coast and submitted a strongly worded complaint about the main induction valve in his sub. In June the Bureau of Construction and Repair replaced the *S-Four*'s valve with a quick-closing model. Savvy promptly submitted a similar request for the *S-Five*, but the Bureau decided to postpone the repair work until after the sub's first mission in the fall. And so, at the end of August, when final adjustments had been completed on her torpedo tubes, the *S-Five* was pronounced seaworthy in spite of her faulty main induction valve.

### TUESDAY, AUGUST 31, 1920, 12:00— SOUTH OF NANTUCKET.

Throughout the morning of the August 31 the *S-Five* ran southwest, spinning out the remainder of the endurance test along the way to Baltimore. At noon Savvy brought his sextant to the bridge in order to check their progress with a sun sight. To be accurate the measurement had to be made at precisely twelve o'clock. Arriving with several minutes to spare, he leaned against the bulwark to look out over the sea. The *S-Five* was churning along at better than twelve knots. With clear skies, the wind astern, and only a moderate sea running, the bridge had become a comfortable place for a change, and the view it afforded of the sub and surrounding ocean was superb.

In Savvy's opinion, when the *S-Five* was cruising at high speed with her decks awash and the long white ribbon of her wake unfurling behind, she was a lovely sight. With his arms folded on the sun-warmed metal, he could feel the deep vibration of her engines and the rhythmic shudder of waves striking against her starboard flank. Blending with the steady rise and fall of the deck, the soothing sensation made the hardened steel seem almost alive.

A few minutes later, while Savvy was completing his sun sight, Charlie Grisham, the sub's executive officer, climbed up to the bridge. A native of Portsmouth, Grisham was what Navy men called a "mustang." That is, instead of earning his officer's commission in the usual fashion by graduating from the Naval Academy, he'd signed on as an enlisted man and worked his way up through the ratings. Just under six feet tall, Charlie was a good-looking fellow, with a broad friendly face and bushy eyebrows that gave him a perpetually surprised look. He was good-natured and energetic, popular with the crew, and, best of all, he knew submarines forwards and backwards, having served on a number of different types during the past three years. A lieutenant jg (for "junior grade") when he'd first come aboard as engineering officer, Charlie had been promoted to lieutenant in the spring and shortly afterward had taken over as the sub's executive officer. Charlie had been especially happy for the pay increase that came with the promotion. He and his wife, Mary, were planning to start a family, and the little house on Langdon Street not far from the railroad tracks in Portsmouth would soon become too small for them.

In June, Grisham's position as junior officer had been taken over by a young ensign fresh out of the Naval Academy. John Bailey Longstaff had transferred in from the heavy cruiser U.S.S. *Huntington*, which had recently arrived in Portsmouth to be decommissioned. Except for his brief time on the *Huntington* and the Naval Academy's summer training cruises, Longstaff had never been to sea. Of medium height, with a slender build, a high forehead and narrow patrician nose, Ensign Longstaff had found life on board a submarine something of a shock, especially after the comparatively roomy quarters on the big cruiser. "My left knee is swollen from the banging I give it every time I drop through the conning tower hatch," he lamented in a letter to his mother back in Nebraska, "But my head is thoroughly deflated. Never have I felt so awkward and useless. Captain Cooke is being very patient with me."

It might have consoled the young officer to know that Captain Cooke considered him to be bright and enthusiastic and expected him to develop into a highly competent submariner once he'd gotten over his inexperience. The same went for the rest of the crew.

Of the thirty-seven enlisted men on the *S-Five*'s roster, fewer than half had been qualified in submarines by the end of the summer and only eight of these had actually served in subs before coming to the *S-Five*. While they were getting up to speed, Savvy felt confident that he and Lieutenant Grisham, along with the boat's fine group of chief petty officers, would be able to keep the submarine running smoothly.

As the Navy's most senior rating, a chief petty officer (CPO) was the military equivalent of middle management, responsible for implementing orders and maintaining liaison between the commissioned officers and the rest of the crew. The *S-Five* had seven CPOs, led by Gunner's Mate Percy Fox, whose seniority and wealth of experience had led Savvy to name him chief of the boat. A tall, heavily-built Midwesterner from a small town in Iowa's corn belt, Fox had been in subs for more than seven years and was by far the most seasoned man in the crew. He'd been assigned to the *S-Five* rather late, coming on board in early June, but by the end of the summer, Savvy had learned to rely on him implicitly. For reasons that Savvy had been unable to discover, the crew gave Fox the nickname "Bubbles."

As for the rest of the enlisted men, except for a couple of "bad apples," as Grisham called them, Savvy considered his crew to be the most likable bunch of sailors he'd found in the Navy. There'd been a few instances of drunkenness and fighting during the summer, mostly with men from other ships, but in general the *S-Five*'s had behaved well. Between March and August Savvy had been obliged to hold "Captain's Mast"—an informal hearing to punish misbehavior by enlisted crewmen—only once, an admirable record for any unit in the Navy.

After exchanging a few words with Grisham, Savvy went below. Celestial navigation wasn't difficult for someone with his mathematical ability; within a few minutes he'd calculated the *S-Five*'s position: about 200 miles southwest of Nantucket. They were exactly on course—but it wasn't the same course that Grisham and Longstaff had laid out over the weekend. At the last moment before sailing on Monday Savvy had discarded their arrow-straight route between the Nantucket Light and the entrance buoy to the Chesapeake Bay. Instead he'd chosen to veer to the northwest, remaining closer to the New England coast. The new route was twelve miles longer than the direct passage, but it kept the sub out of the busy deepwater shipping lanes that ran further out at sea. Savvy wanted the crew to concentrate on their performance during the testing instead of worrying about being run down by a steamship. In addition he suspected that the men handling the diving controls might be more aggressive, if there were only a couple of hundred feet of water beneath them instead several thousand. He couldn't know it yet, but this course change would become the most fateful decision he'd ever made.

At 2:00 the first endurance run came to an end and Savvy ordered Grisham and Percy Fox to make the boat ready to dive. Ten minutes later the *S-Five* slipped smoothly underwater. By 2:15 she'd been trimmed down to a depth of fifty feet and was running at a steady eight knots, still maintaining her course toward the Chesapeake.

The transition from surface to underwater cruising was always striking. Unless there was a storm topside, wave action seldom extended below periscope depth, so the sub ran smoothly and quietly.

After the clamor of the diesels, the muted hum of the electric drive motors was a welcome change. Throughout the remainder of the afternoon the big Westinghouse power plants purred steadily, while the electricians recorded current and voltage readings for the test reports. Five hours after she'd submerged, at the conclusion of endurance run, Savvy had the *S-Five* brought back to the surface.

There was a strict protocol for surfacing, designed to minimize the likelihood of collisions. Savvy had the *S-Five* brought to periscope depth. When she was level at forty feet, he raised the wide-angle periscope and searched for activity on the surface, pivoting slowly in a circle as he turned the scope through 360 degrees. Only then did he give the order to surface.

It was essential to come up quickly at this point, because the periscope extended only a few feet above the surface, allowing Savvy to see no more than a few miles in any direction. A fast-moving ship could cover that distance in minutes. The moment that the conning tower broke through the surface, the lookout popped the hatch and scrambled topside, followed by the officer of the deck—Savvy in this case—and the two of them quickly scanned the surrounding sea for any sign of danger.

It was just before moonrise. Seen by starlight, the Atlantic seemed to stretch limitlessly in all directions. There was no sign of another vessel. Savvy was pleased. Although not as demanding as the diving procedures, the surfacing routine was important, and the crew had carried it off nicely. As soon as the sub had been switched over to diesel power, he ordered the electricians to re-configure the drive motors to act as generators. For the remainder of the night the *S-Five* would cruise slowly along the surface, using most of the power from her diesels to recharge the batteries. Shortly after they'd gotten under way again, the moon rose. One day past full, it flooded the ocean with light, paving their way south toward Baltimore.

Although Savvy was still concerned about the main induction valve, he soon acquired another, and potentially more serious, problem. Not long after the *S-Five* had surfaced, while the elec-tric motors were being rewired, the engineering watch reported that one of the cylinder heads in the port diesel engine had cracked.

This wasn't the first time the *S-Five* had needed mending. From March until May she'd been without her high-resolution periscope, while its watertight sleeve was replaced. In June one of the other submarines at the Yard had fouled the *S-Five*'s pro-pellers at dockside, causing extensive damage, and in July one of her starboard cylinder heads had cracked. In each case the repair work had been straightforward but time-consuming, and it was this aspect of the current damage that bothered Savvy. If the *S-Five*'s power plant held up until she reached Baltimore, local re-pair facilities could replace the cracked head during the layover with no harm done; but, if not, Savvy and his men would have to repair the engine at sea or limp along on reduced power. In either case, they'd fall behind schedule, perhaps even have to skip one of the cities on their route. Such a failure during their first assignment would be a grave embarrassment, no matter what the cause.

In spite of these vexations, Savvy saw no reason to complain about his new command. Equipment failures were an accepted part of a submarine captain's lot in 1920 and impromptu repairs were often required to keep boats at sea. With the exception of the main induction valve and the cylinder head, the S-Five's performance record had been exemplary. Taking everything into consideration, Savvy felt lucky to captain such a splendid new sub.

As her name implied, the S-Five was the fifth of the Navy's new S-Class submarines. With a length of 231 feet and a displacement of 870 tons she was also the largest. Her armament was formidable: four twenty-one-inch torpedo tubes in her forward compartment enabled her to launch fan-shaped torpedo salvos that enemy ships found hard to evade, while a four-inch deck gun forward of the conning tower gave her additional firepower on the surface. Her twin propellers were driven by 1,000-horsepower diesel engines that could speed her at better than fifteen knots on the surface, while her two 600-horsepower electric motors could produce eleven knots submerged. Thanks to her extra-large fuel tanks, capable of holding nearly 37,000 gallons of diesel oil, she had an extended cruising range of over 5,000 miles, more than any other submarine in the fleet.

As for the cracked cylinder head, there was no point in worrying about it. The engines had performed well so far in spite of the damage. The only *sure* way to avert trouble during tomorrow's speed run was to abort it altogether.

WEDNESDAY, SEPTEMBER 1, 1920, 09:00—
OFF NEW YORK.

Wednesday morning dawned clear and cool, with a crisp northwest breeze and a moderate sea out of the north. When Savvy
climbed up to the bridge, the sun had cleared the horizon and was
burning away the last of the morning's haze. The *S-Five* was cruising toward the southwest at a modest speed, barely enough to
maintain steerage in the swells. By 9:40 the batteries had been
fully charged. Savvy sent word below to make ready for high-
speed running. At 9:48 the engine room reported that the motor
armatures had been rewired for power and the diesels were ready
for full throttle.

The air was crisp and invigorating, and the waves smacking into
the *S-Five*'s side sent tremors through her hull, as if she were a thor-
oughbred quivering on the start line. The tension on the bridge reflected emotions throughout the sub. If the port diesel maintained
compression for the next four hours, they'd probably be home free.

Savvy glanced at his wristwatch; it read 9:50. Bending low over
the conning tower hatch, he shouted, "All ahead, port and starboard."

Below him the helmsman pulled the engine room telegraph
levers over and back, stopping at *Ahead Full.* "All ahead, port and
starboard, Aye," he echoed.

There was a muffled cough from below deck as the diesels
surged into life. Gouts of black smoke puffed out of the exhaust
ports along the side of the hull. The sea astern began to boil as the
sub's propellers turned faster. Minutes later the helmsman reported that the *S-Five* was making fifteen knots. She was charging
across the sea now, her bow throwing up curtains of spray that the
wind tore into tatters and whisked away. Spreading far out on either side, the bow wave merged with the propeller wash into a
wide white swath that stretched for miles astern.

When they'd reached cruising speed, Savvy went below to inspect the engine room. As he climbed down through the conning
tower hatch, he could feel the powerful rush of air being drawn

into the sub by the engines. Even with the additional ventilation provided by the main induction valve, the big diesels used so much air that they created a palpable breeze through the sub. Small wonder that timing was so critical during a dive. If ventilation were cut off too early, the engines could create a partial vacuum inside the sub. Savvy had heard of instances in which this had actually affected the hearing of crew members.

If the control room was noisy, it was nothing compared to the racket inside the engine room. Bill Bender, the chief machinist's mate in charge of the morning watch, climbed down from the catwalk to report. According to Bender the port diesel was running well, with no sign of power loss due to the cracked head. A few minutes later, Savvy climbed back up to the conning tower, his ears still ringing from the noise. When he emerged topside the cool sea air was startling after the heavy reek of oil and exhaust fumes below.

One more hurdle remained, but it wasn't the underwater speed run, which Savvy expected to go without a hitch. It was the crash dive. Everyone on board was conscious of it, as a matter of pride in their boat. The performance tests were part of a yearly Navy-wide competition between ships. The scores were cumulative. Every second over the one-minute time limit in the upcoming crash dive would result in a penalty point for the *S-Five*.

Of course, the scores weren't the real issue. What counted was the submarine's capability. If the *S-Five* ever went into combat, an efficient quick dive might someday be the only thing standing between her and destruction. Savvy and his crew were practicing for the real thing.

WHEN THE *S-Five*'s sea trials began in May, training for her crew started in earnest too. During the following weeks short cruises out into the Atlantic became two- or three-day jaunts to Boston, New London, and Provincetown. After months of tedious dockside labor, the crew quickly learned to enjoy these excursions, but more importantly they began to learn how to handle the *S-Five*.

The first order of business was to familiarize themselves with surface navigation, since this was what they'd do most when they were on patrol. Unlike modern nuclear boats, which can remain underwater for months at a time, submarines of the World War I era spent most of their time on the surface, submerging only when necessary to avoid detection or to engage the enemy.

The day came when the *S-Fives* had to make their first dive. It was a protracted affair, as Savvy, Charlie Grisham, and the chiefs walked their inexperienced crew through the procedure called "trimming down." This was the gradual technique used during routine dives, when speed wasn't of prime importance. Its step-by-step nature allowed crew members to concentrate on the individual principles of diving.

The first of these was *buoyancy,* which had been known since the third century B.C., when the Greek philosopher Archimedes realized that changing an object's weight without changing its volume would make it sink or float. In 1776 David Bushnell's egg-shaped submersible, the *Turtle,* was equipped with a hand-powered pump to change its buoyancy by moving seawater in and out of its hull. Modern submarines use the same method to change that buoyancy, although the details differ. For example, there is evidence that Bushnell's working model didn't provide a separate chamber for the water, which simply ran to the bottom of the hull around the operator's feet.

In order to keep their occupants dry, modern subs are equipped with large steel reservoirs, called ballast tanks, attached to the outside of the pressure hull. The *S-Five* had six main ballast tanks, arranged in pairs along either side: forward, amidships, and aft with fuel and fresh water tanks mounted between them. By adjusting the amount of seawater in one tank or another, the sub's center of buoyancy could be shifted to keep the sub on an even keel. An additional large ballast tank, called the safety tank, was kept flooded at all times in order to provide reserve buoyancy in emergencies.

Water entered and left the ballast tanks through large valves called Kingstons in the bottom of each tank. These valves were operated through a system of long, jointed tie rods connecting them to rows of waist-high levers at the aft end of the control room. Direct mechanical linkages like this were common in submarines of this era, despite the fact that they were notoriously hard to operate. The Kingstons on the *S-Five* were so intractable that several men were often needed to open or close a single valve.

The second principle of diving was introduced to modern subs by Simon Lake, the New Jersey born inventor who competed with John Holland for control of the American submarine market. An inveterate tinkerer, Lake contributed a number of important advances, one of the most useful of which was diving rudders, called hydroplanes today. Mounted on either side of a sub, diving rudders could be angled to direct its motion either up or down. The *S-Five* had two sets of diving rudders, a pair near the bow and another near the stern. They were folded against the hull during surface cruising and extended by means of hand cranks prior to dives, after which their angle was set from the control room.

Both ballast tanks and diving rudders were used when a sub was "trimmed down." After the diving signal was made the Kingston valves were opened, allowing seawater to flow into the ballast tanks. As the sub's buoyancy decreased, the diving rudders were extended and angled a few degrees so as to deflect her forward motion downward. Within several minutes she would gradually "sail" herself underwater, traveling a mile or more in the process, depending on her speed. What the method lacked in rapidity it more than made up for in safety and control.

The same could not be said for crash dives, which employed the same two principles of diving to quite different effect.

Savvy could still recall the *S-Five*'s first *crash* dive. It had taken place on July 1 and, while not necessarily a disaster, had not been a success either. The crew had been accustomed to a regular sequence of orders during dives: "Open forward Kingstons," "Four degrees down rudder," "Make all watertight," and so on. But there was no such leisurely approach in a crash dive. Every man had to perform multiple tasks without prompting and with split-second precision: no orders, no reports, and no room for error. That first dive had taken four minutes and eighteen seconds. Three months and more than forty dives later, the crew had improved greatly, but, as their times indicated, they still had a lot to learn.

# 2

# CRASH DIVE!

"Every great mistake has a halfway moment, a split second when it can be recalled and perhaps remedied."
— PEARL S. BUCK

WEDNESDAY, SEPTEMBER 1, 1920, 11:45—
OFF NEW JERSEY.

A few minutes before noon, members of the third section spread through the *S-Five* to relieve the morning watch. Waiting on the bridge to take another sun sight, Savvy smiled as he listened to the helmsman for the afternoon watch taking report on the steering platform below him. The *S-Five*'s crew hailed from all over the country, representing fully half of the forty-eight states. Although Savvy knew all of his men by sight, he could recognize only a few of them by their voices; but Quartermaster[1] George Bill, the helmsman coming on for the third watch, came from Yonkers, and his thick New York accent was a dead giveaway.

A short time later Savvy was at the chart table in the control room working out the noon sight. His reckoning gave the *S-Five*'s position as latitude 38.30 North and longitude 74.03 West, putting

[1] Although sailors from many different specialties could—and often did—serve as steersmen on Navy ships, the official rating for a helmsman was "Quartermaster."

them about forty-five miles east of the entrance to the Delaware Bay. He transcribed the coordinates into the logbook with satisfaction. The *S-Five* was still on course and making good time, too. With a little more than 250 miles to go, they might reach Baltimore by midday Thursday, leaving plenty of time to make the boat shipshape for Friday's visitors and give the crew liberty that evening too.

In the engine room Bill Bender had just been relieved by Chief Gunner's Mate Russell Hutson. "Reb" Hutson came from a small town near Hampton Roads in the tidewater section of Virginia. His nickname reflected his pride in being the only member of the crew native to the "Old Dominion." With less than two hours to go in the morning's speed run, Bender reported that the diesels were holding up well.

On his way back though the control room Savvy stopped to speak with Percy Fox. Besides being chief of the boat, Fox was also in charge of the third watch. Typically he positioned himself near the center of the control room "to make sure everything's running good when we dive the boat." Although his lack of formal education was evident in his speech, Fox was one of the most knowledgeable men on board in the ways of subs; and he took his responsibilities seriously.


### 13:30—The Bridge.

By the time Savvy reached the bridge again, it was 1:30. Charlie Grisham had come up for a breath of fresh air, giving Savvy the opportunity to discuss the impending dive with his executive officer. Grisham expressed confidence that they'd break the two-minute mark today, but Savvy preferred to reserve judgment. He'd been disappointed before.

With less than twenty minutes to go before the crash dive, Savvy decided it was time to let the sub "ride on her vents." To his surprise Grisham volunteered to carry the order below in person, rather than relaying it via the helmsman on the steering platform;

but after a moment's reflection he understood. The exec wanted to keep a close eye on things during the dive.

Officially Ensign Longstaff was in charge of the control room during the third watch, but so far in his brief career, he'd overseen barely a half dozen dives. With Chief Fox to help him, the young officer might carry out today's crash dive briskly enough, but with Charlie Grisham there to back them both up, there was an even better chance that the maneuver would go well. During his time in the service, Grisham had carried out hundreds of dives in all kinds of conditions.

When Savvy told Charlie to go ahead, the exec slid down the ladder to the steering platform and disappeared through the lower hatch. A few minutes later Savvy dismissed the bridge watch. Slinging his binoculars around his neck, the sailor climbed down from his perch behind the periscope struts and followed Grisham, leaving Savvy alone on the bridge.

Letting the sub "ride on her vents" was Navy slang for a way to flood the ballast tanks quickly. The Kingston valves worked far too slowly for this; if a crash dive were started with the Kingstons closed, they could never be opened in time. So they were opened *before* the dive, which meant that the only thing keeping seawater out of the ballast tanks was the air trapped inside them, just as the air in a drinking glass keeps it from filling when it's inverted under water.

Each pair of ballast tanks shared a common air vent located in the compartment above them. At the signal for a crash dive, men stationed at the vents spun them open, allowing the air in the ballast tanks to escape from the top and seawater to flood in at the bottom. The arrangement made diving faster, because the air vents could be opened much more quickly than the Kingstons. Poised like this, with Kingstons open and air vents closed, a submarine was said to be "riding on her vents."

### 13:40—Control Room.

It was a good thing he'd come below, Charlie Grisham thought ten minutes later. When the Kingstons had been opened, he'd noticed that the sub began riding lower than she should have. Something was letting water into the ballast tanks. A quick check revealed that the forward main air vent hadn't sealed properly. The vent was located in the battery room. By the time Charlie had identified the culprit and closed it, the S-*Five* had taken on a good deal of water. She'd also developed a distinct *list*—or tilt—to starboard. Evidently the swells breaking against the sub's starboard quarter had caused more water to enter on that side.

That was the trouble with having a common air vent for both port and starboard tanks, Charlie reflected, as he hurried back to the control room. The only way to regulate the tanks individually was to adjust the Kingstons, which was always difficult. Nevertheless, if he and his shipmates wanted to do well in the crash dive today, they couldn't afford to start it with the boat canted over to one side.

When Charlie reached the control room, he asked Percy Fox to "bear a hand" with the Kingstons. The big chief petty officer hurried over to help. The easiest way to rebalance the sub at this point was to close the starboard Kingstons and open the port ones further. Together the two men wrestled with the stubborn control levers, going more by feel and instinct than by any particular plan, until the S-*Five* was nearly upright.

While Grisham and Fox dealt with the Kingstons and the members of the third watch prepared for the crash dive, many of their crewmates "hit the rack." With three sections to stand watch, sailors spent a third of their time on duty, in addition to any other responsibilities they might have. And on a submarine *everyone* had extra responsibilities. Consequently few off-duty sailors passed up an opportunity to catch some shut-eye. Because the battery room was the quietest place in the boat, they usually grabbed bunks there, whether they'd been assigned to them or not. For many of the older hands this was nothing new. In the smaller subs they'd known it was often customary to assign several sailors to each berth in a rotating system called "hot bunking."

Chief Machinist's Mate Fred "Shipmate" Whitehead spent the morning at his regular duty station in the engine room tending the throttles for the diesels. Fred's *emergency* station was at the "air manifold" in the control room, which meant that during the upcoming dive, his counterpart in the third watch would have to secure the throttles and then hustle up to the control room in time to carry out his duties there. Fred knew from experience how difficult this could be. And so shortly before two o'clock he rose from his bunk and strolled down to the control room to set up the air manifold for the dive.

Fred Whitehead was another of the *S-Five's* most accomplished hands. Like Charlie Grisham, he'd served in subs during the war, including a tour in the North Sea, during which he'd met a pretty young English nurse named Dorothy. After the war Fred had returned to England, married Dorothy, and brought her back to America. That was last November. Now Dorothy was pregnant with their first child. The last time he'd heard from her, she was staying with his parents in Brooklyn, because she wasn't feeling well. Fred was eager to reach Baltimore, so that he could telephone her and find out how she was doing. In the meantime he didn't mind staying busy. He wouldn't have slept much anyway.

The *air manifold* was an array of valves and gauges on the control room's forward bulkhead. It regulated he sub's compressed air system, which consisted of three large *storage banks,* two powerful *compressors* in the motor room, and a network of high-pressure tubing to carry the air throughout the sub. All of these components were linked through the air manifold, making it one of the most important control centers in the sub.

Compressed air was useful in many ways, from running pumps to launching torpedoes; but, as Fred emphasized to novices, one application outweighed all the others: forcing water out of the ballast tanks (called "blowing" the tanks) in order to get the sub to the surface after a dive.

The gauges showed that all three air banks were at their maximum capacity of 2,250 p.s.i. Fred pressurized the rest of the system by opening master valves on the first two banks. From there he fed the air through a "stepdown manifold" to reduce its pressure to a more useful 90 p.s.i. When the needle on the downstream pressure gauge twitched up into the green band, Fred stepped back. He was done. Casting his eye around the control room, he saw other members of the crew running through their own checklists. At the aft end of the compartment, Lieutenant Grisham and Chief Fox were struggling with the control levers for the Kingstons, no doubt trying to correct the list that had developed during the past few minutes.

Fred didn't fool himself. His preparations at the air manifold were important, but they represented only a small fraction of the steps necessary for a successful dive. And, while he could prime the air manifold ahead of time, many crewmen had to perform their duties during the dive itself.

Two of those chores were of paramount importance. The first was the power transition. At the moment the sub slipped below the surface the engine room gang had to shut down the diesels and disengage them from the propeller shafts. Simultaneously the electricians in the control room had to feed current to the big drive motors that turned the screws underwater. This shift from diesel to electrical power required exquisite timing. If the motors were started too *soon*, while the diesels were still engaged, the power train could be damaged. On the other hand, if the motors were started too *late*, the sub would lose propulsion during the most critical part of the dive.

Only one other task was as important as the power transition during a dive: making the boat watertight. From the klaxon's first shrill blast, crewmen throughout the sub had to close a myriad of openings, both large and small, in the sub's steel pressure hull.

Some of these openings, like the cooling vents for the ice machine, could be closed ahead of time. Others, like the main ventilation system, could not!

The *S-Five* had two main sources of ventilation during surface cruising: the conning tower hatch and the main induction valve. On a big boat like the *S-Five* both of these had to remain open until the last possible moment during a dive, for if they were closed too early, the sub's huge engines would suck down much of the air in the hull. On the other hand, if they were left open too long, even a few seconds, they could cause dangerous flooding.

To avoid catastrophic mistakes either way only the most reliable people in each watch were given responsibility for the ventilation systems. During today's dive Savvy himself would handle the conning tower hatch, while down in the control room Percy Fox would take care of the main induction valve. The skipper and the chief of the boat. Surely it would have been hard to choose two more trustworthy people for these all-important duties. As he stood on the bridge that afternoon, waiting for Grisham to give the go-ahead for the dive, Savvy must have felt confident that the exercise would go well.

## 13:40—Steering Platform.

Quartermaster George Bill was a relative newcomer to the *S-Five*, having joined the crew in mid-June, but he'd quickly proved himself to be the most reliable steersman on board, which was probably why he'd been tapped to man the helm during today's crash dive. As the speed run drew to a close in the early afternoon, Bill stayed busy relaying information back and forth. The speaking tubes to the bridge ended on the steering platform, where they were protected by the upper conning tower hatch, making him the last link in the chain of communication.

With about twenty minutes remaining before the dive, Lieutenant Grisham slid down from the bridge and continued through the lower hatch into the control room. Fifteen minutes later the voice tube emitted a shrill whistle. Bill pulled out the stop and put his ear to the tube. A moment later he hailed the bridge: "Control room calling, Sir. Mr. Grisham reports speed run complete . . ."

### 13:40—Torpedo Room.

Gunner's Mate First Class Henry Love sat on an empty packing case. When the klaxon horn sounded, it would be his job to turn the hand crank that extended the forward diving rudders. Once they had been "rigged out," he could relax until the *S-Five* reached cruising depth, when he might have to operate one or two of the small "trim tanks" that were used to fine-tune the sub's buoyancy.

No one slept in the torpedo room during this watch, so Henry had the place to himself, which was just as he liked it. A stocky New Englander, he came from the old whaling port of Bedford, Massachusetts, at one time one of the wealthiest cities in the world because of its control of the tea trade. During the summer he'd been transferred for six weeks to another submarine, the *S-Four,* where he'd been assigned to a more crowded watch station. It had been a relief to get back to the *S-Five* and his solitary torpedo room vigil.

### 13:40—Engine Room.

Electrician First Class Frank Peters leaned against the engine room railing and rubbed his eyes. Hot, noisy, reeking of oil and diesel fumes, this was the last place he'd normally want to be after working all morning in the control room; but he'd volunteered to help. The engineers were spread thin during crash dives, especially those involving tests, because of all the data that had to be collected. Many of them had to rush off to dive stations elsewhere in the boat and didn't have time to record things like engine turns, the job that Frank had offered to do.

Frank wasn't the only volunteer. Up on the catwalk he could

see John Smith, a machinist's mate from the morning watch, standing by at the throttles. Smith was talking with Chief Bender, who'd just been relieved, but apparently Bender was sticking around too. That impressed Frank even more. After four hours nursing these hot, noisy diesels, Bender must be worn out; yet there he was on the catwalk, coaching one of his sailors through the shutdown procedures.

In spite of the racket, it was hard to stay awake, so Frank passed the time talking with one of the engineers. Admittedly it wasn't much of a conversation. The roar of engines made normal speech impossible; people communicated here mainly by shouting in each other's ears and making gestures. As far as Frank could tell, the engineer was grumbling about having slept through lunch. Although he tried to look interested, Frank could feel his attention wandering.

Frank Bernard Peters came from Watertown, a small city at the eastern end of Lake Ontario, where he lived with his wife, Jessie. In addition to his duties as an electrician, Frank also served as the sub's radio operator. Radios had been standard equipment on Navy ships since 1900, but the technology hadn't evolved as rapidly as the ships themselves. State-of-the-art radio equipment in 1920 used powerful vacuum tube amplifiers to send and receive voice transmissions; but most shipboard radios still relied on old-fashioned spark-gap transmitters and crystal receivers that could handle only Morse Code. In July, while the *S-Five* had been stationed temporarily in Provincetown, Frank had been able to try out a new underwater transmitter on loan from the General Electric company. The device had been able to send radio signals underwater far better than any crystal set he'd ever used, sometimes from as deep as twenty feet. He'd been sorry to see it go. Something like that might come in handy in an emergency.

13:53—Steering Platform.

" . . . All stations manned and ready," George Bill finished his report to the captain.

There was a momentary pause. The skipper was probably taking a last look around. Then the order came loud and clear: "Dive! Dive!"

Bill immediately set the port and starboard engine telegraphs to "Stop" and triggered the dive alarm. The klaxon horn began to wail and Bill stepped quickly out of the way, as the captain came hurtling down from the bridge, his feet sliding along the outside of the ladder. Bill was already tugging on the wire lanyard that would close the upper hatch. This never worked easily, because the hatch cover was held open by a powerful coil spring in its hinge to keep it from slamming back and forth when the sub rolled; but today it wouldn't move at all, even when both Bill and Cooke put their weight on it. Peering up, they saw that the lanyard had snarled around the hatch cover.

The sub had already started down; Bill could feel the deck sloping beneath his feet. Within seconds the sea would reach the top of the conning tower and spill over into the bridge. Bill could picture dark water pouring over the gunwale and down into the sub. Boats had been lost this way! He scrambled up the ladder and jerked hard on the lanyard, while the Captain pulled again from below. This time the hatch cover slammed shut. Bill spun the locking wheel until it stopped. "Hatch secure, sir," he said, but by the time he'd uttered "sir," Cooke had vanished through the lower hatch into the control room.

Turning back to the three-foot-diameter steering wheel, Bill glanced at the binnacle, the bowl-shaped housing that contained the ship's compass. According to the circular compass card inside it, the S-Five was on a heading of 219 degrees true, only one degree off her assigned course. Satisfied, Bill looked through the forward porthole, where he could see the bow diving planes biting into the waves. So far the dive seemed to be going well in spite of the brief problem with the hatch. Bill nodded approvingly. Like all good seamen, he took pride in his vessel's performance. Besides, a good time on the dive today might mean extra liberty in their next port of call. Bill and his shipmates had heard intriguing rumors of theater parties and other festivities that the host cities had planned for their visits.

Bill checked the compass again, saw that the sub had fallen several degrees off course, and automatically adjusted the wheel to compensate. Keeping an eye on the binnacle, he waited for the compass card to swing back to the correct heading, but instead it drifted even farther. Bill shifted the wheel again, but the sub still failed to respond. It was time to report the problem. Turning toward the lower hatch he yelled to get the attention of the sailor normally stationed at the foot of the ladder. "She's not answering her helm," he called. "Tell the captain."

There was no answer. Stooping farther, Bill peered through the hatchway. The sailor was standing in water! As Bill stared in stunned silence, several boxes floated past and an awful realization began to dawn on him.

### 13:53—Torpedo Room.

As soon as the klaxon sounded, Henry Love jumped to his feet and began turning the hand crank for the diving rudders. When he'd finished, he leaned back against the bulkhead to rest, trying to picture the sub's bow plowing down into the sea only a few yards away. It was a fascinating image. The dive seemed to be going faster than usual. Maybe they'd break that one-minute record that everyone kept talking about.

Love's thoughts were interrupted by a muffled growl coming from somewhere aft. He cocked his head, trying to identify the noise, and was about to get up and walk back to the battery room to ask about it, when a shaft of clear green water lanced down into the compartment behind him. Splattering from the bulkheads and torpedoes, it filled the air with a blinding salt spray that stung Henry's eyes. He lurched to his feet and swung around to locate the source. Finally by shielding his face with his forearm he discovered that the water was coming in through the big overhead ventilator near the rear of the compartment. Stumbling to the doorway, he shouted that the torpedo room was taking in water, then slogged back to try to stop it.

### 13:53—Engine Room.

Fifteen minutes after Lieutenant Grisham breezed through the engine room on his pre-dive inspection, the telegraph rang "All Stop" and the klaxon began to howl. The compartment exploded into activity. Chief Bender pulled the telegraph lever over and back to confirm the order from the bridge. John Smith began to cut back on the throttles. The engineer to whom Frank had been talking threw in the engine clutches to disconnect them from the propeller shafts, locked them, and hurried off to his dive station in the control room. Meanwhile the engine room gang began closing the valves and ports that would make the boat watertight.

Twenty seconds after the dive alarm had sounded, the big diesels rattled to a halt. Frank leaned over the guardrail around the starboard diesel, squinting at the grimy engine counters, and jotted the number of engine turns onto a scrap of paper. After repeating the process for the port diesel, he climbed back down onto the central catwalk and started toward the control room with the paper slip in his hand. Once he'd submitted these readings, he'd have done his bit and could get some rest.

With a rumbling hiss a dark emerald curtain dropped across the catwalk in front of him, sluiced through the steel grating and spattered into the bilges. Steam billowed up as water sizzled on the hot exhaust manifolds. Frank jumped backed instinctively, but in the same instant he realized he couldn't remain here. As the sub's only qualified radioman, his place during an emergency was in the control room—on the other side of that olivine wall. There was no time to debate the issue. Stuffing the slip of paper into his pocket, Frank lowered his head and charged straight into the down-rushing column.

## 13:53—Control Room.

When Savvy reached the bottom of the conning tower ladder, he found Fred Whitehead at the air manifold calmly checking gauges. That was reassuring. With Whitehead on duty here, Savvy had one less thing to worry about. As he started aft, he could see Charlie Grisham at the far end of the compartment standing beside the Kingstons. The exec looked somewhat disheveled, small wonder considering how hard he must have worked to adjust them.

Savvy edged past the main switchboard on the starboard side of the control room. Once the clutch telegraph had told the electricians that it was safe to go ahead, they'd use the big rheostats there to send current to the drive motors. On the port side of the control room, directly across from the switchboard, were the diving rudder controls, a pair of vertical hand wheels the size of bicycle tires with matching depth gauges and angle indicators above them. This was Savvy's goal. During the sea trials in July, he'd learned how important it was to control the *S-Five*'s angle of descent. A steep angle produced a faster dive, but when the stern rose higher than fifteen degrees, the propellers came out of the water and the resulting loss of speed more than offset the advantage of a steep dive. In addition, when the dive angle was too great, the boat tended to overshoot its target depth, which was both time consuming and potentially dangerous.

Eventually Savvy had decided to coach the man at the diving rudders throughout each dive; but today he found Percy Fox manning the controls, and it looked as though the big chief petty officer had already adjusted them to the correct angle. Savvy couldn't have been more pleased. Because of the delay with the conning tower hatch he'd gotten to the control room later than usual, but two of his most trusted CPOs had filled in at critical dive stations and everything seemed to have gone smoothly in spite of his absence.

Savvy checked the time on his stopwatch. A little less than forty seconds had elapsed since he'd given the order to dive. At the main switchboard the electricians had energized the port drive motor and were waiting for the signal to go ahead on the starboard side. Everything seemed to be in order. The *S-Five* wouldn't break the one minute mark today, but she'd still have a respectable time.

The rudder man for the third watch hurried up from his previous post and Percy Fox stood up to relinquish the controls. By now the deck had taken on a slant of about ten degrees. Savvy turned toward the inclinometers to check the exact reading. He never got to see it.

Without warning a huge stream of water plunged down from the overhead, struck the deck beside Savvy and blossomed into a flower of icy spray. For an instant everyone in the control room froze, staring at the apparition with expressions of shock and disbelief. One face in particular wore a look of anguish that confirmed Savvy's first incredulous thought. Percy Fox, the chief of the boat, the senior enlisted man aboard, and the last person Savvy would have expected to make such a mistake, had forgotten his primary duty. He'd allowed the *S-Five* to submerge with her main induction valve wide open. Now a sixteen-inch column of water was pouring in through the ventilation system, driven by the momentum of 870 tons of steel traveling at fifteen knots through the sea.

13:55—Torpedo Room.

The shut-off valve for the ventilator outlet was located above the starboard rank of torpedoes, too high for Henry Love to reach while standing on the deck. Using one of the torpedo racks as a step, he struggled up onto the topmost torpedo. Then, straddling the thick steel tube as if it were a horse, he reached blindly over head into the stream of water and groped for the control wheel. Even when he finally found it, the wheel was nearly impossible to turn. The torpedoes were covered with a layer of grease to protect them against water and rust, and the slippery coating had covered his hands, making it difficult for him to grasp anything. The grease made it hard for him to maintain his position on the torpedo too. Holding on to the frame of a nearby bunk, he tried to overpower the wheel one-handed, but it was hard to get any leverage.

As if things weren't bad enough, water began spraying around the valve stem into Henry's face with such force that he had to let go of the wheel periodically and lean out to the side in order to breathe. Nevertheless, the wheel was moving, if only gradually. Henry knew that it took twelve full turns to close the valve. He wasn't sure how many he'd made by now, but it wasn't enough. As the water continued to pound him and the cold began to sap his strength, he wondered if he'd last long enough to close the valve. Or if anyone had heard his call for help.

"Hank! You've gotta get out of there!"

Blinking the water out of his eyes (and nearly falling from the torpedo) Love peered over his shoulder. Someone was wading toward him. Wading? He looked down. To his horror water had not only covered the deck, it had risen to the top of the lower torpedo tubes, barely an inch below the sill of the battery room doorway!

"Come on!" It was one of the chiefs, shouting at him again, "The compartment's gonna flood! We've got to secure this door!"

Henry's thoughts tumbled over each other. If they evacuated the torpedo room and shut the watertight door, before he'd closed the valve completely, the compartment would flood. But, if they didn't, water would spill through into the battery room. Like everyone else on board, Henry knew the consequences of flooded batteries: power failure, poisonous gas. . . . He looked at the water pouring in through the ventilator. It hadn't decreased appreciably. By now the torpedo room resounded with the deep rumble of a giant bathtub being filled. Reluctantly he slid off the torpedo into the waist-deep water and followed the chief toward the aft bulkhead.

13:55—Engine Room.

Frank hit the water at a dead run. The impact on his back and shoulders staggered him, but he grabbed the catwalk's railing with both hands, stayed on his feet, and pulled himself through to the other side. Looking back over his shoulder, he saw one of the engine room gang—a fireman, he thought—try to follow. The water drove the burly sailor down onto his knees, then knocked him sprawling back between the engines.

For the first time Frank was able to see the source of the flooding; it was coming in through the main ventilator outlet directly above the catwalk, pouring down in an apparently unstoppable flood; but Hutson and Smith had vaulted across the catwalk's guard rail and were tugging on the hand wheel beside the outlet. Frank couldn't wait to see if they'd succeed. He was about to turn and slip through the forward bulkhead into the control room, when the strangest thing happened.

Before the engineers had turned the control wheel nearly enough to close the valve, the water began to taper off on its own. Within seconds it had stopped entirely. Peering up into the dripping ventilator shaft, Chief Hutson grunted and declared that the intense water pressure in the pipe must have collapsed the valve stem. *Which meant that the water was probably being diverted further aft.* Without a word, Smith turned and dashed along the catwalk toward the motor room.

Frank had seen enough. Even if the immediate danger was past here, he still had to get to the radio shack. There was no telling what messages the skipper might need to send once the sub had reached the surface; and there was no doubt in Frank's mind that Captain Cooke would head back up, once things had stabilized. Ducking his head, he swung himself through the doorway into the control room.

And found himself back in the middle of chaos.

## 13:55—Control Room.

"Rudders to hard rise!" Savvy bellowed. "Blow main tanks! Blow safety."

Without waiting to see if his orders were being carried out, he lunged for the big overhead hand-wheel for the main induction valve. Hanging on to it with both hands, he jerked and twisted as hard as he could, but the valve, the same stubborn mechanism that should have been replaced in June, refused to budge. Moments later Fox and Grisham joined him, but not even their added strength could turn the wheel.

On the other side of the compartment a shower of sparks exploded from the main electrical panel as salt water found its way into the wiring. Circuit breakers blew in a succession of sharp cracks and the boat's lighting flickered wildly until the emergency circuits took over. As Savvy heaved at the wheel, he felt something cold on his ankles. Looking down he saw that water had risen above the deck plates. The bilges had filled already! Hundreds of gallons of water in less than a minute!

Above the drumming of the water on the deck the shouts of the men were barely audible, but most of the crew fought for their lives in silence. Yelling would have been a waste of breath. Chief Whitehead had already sent men to close the air vents. Now he crouched at the air manifold, running through the valve sequences that would send compressed air into the ballast tanks. The electricians danced back and forth in front of the main switchboard, closing breakers, replacing fuses, rerouting circuits, trying anything that might restore the electrical system.

In a tangled knot near the center of the control room, Savvy, Percy Fox, and Charlie Grisham grappled with the main induction valve. As far as Savvy could tell, the wheel hadn't moved. The stream of water pouring through the ventilator outlet looked as thick as a tree trunk. Then he remembered that the outlet itself was equipped with a flapper valve. If he could close that, it would stop the flooding here in the control room, even if they couldn't overpower the central valve. Splashing across the deck to the outlet, he groped upward to find the control lever and the heavy wing nut that locked it in place, but the force of the water knocked him down. By the time he'd regained his feet Grisham was beside him. Together they forced their way up into the stream, loosened the wing nut and pulled the control lever down. The flooding stopped.

In the ensuing stillness the smallest sounds seemed unusually loud: water dripping, men panting, electrical systems crackling. Water was everywhere, tracing rivulets down bulkheads, pooling in hollows and crevices, ankle deep on the deck. It was dark too, because the auxiliary lights only produced about half normal illumination. Men were still working on the main induction valve. Percy Fox had stuck a twenty-four-inch Stillson wrench through the spokes of the hand wheel and was hauling on it, cursing steadily under his breath, but they didn't make much headway until Grisham splashed back to lend a hand. Then the wheel finally began to inch around. When it would turn no further, they stepped back, out of breath and soaked to the skin.

### 13:57—Torpedo Room.

The flooring in the battery room was built up several feet to accommodate the battery wells, so Henry Love and the Chief had to climb a set of steps to reach the doorway. When he reached the bottom of the steps, Henry turned back.

"Wait a sec, Chief!" he yelled.

Moving to the port side of the compartment, he took a deep breath, ducked underwater and fumbled around behind the lowest torpedo for the valve that controlled the aft bilge drains. When he found at last, he opened it all the way and then, gasping and choking again, climbed up the steps and through the doorway into the battery room. He helped the chief close the watertight door and dog it shut, then leaned against the bulkhead, feeling utterly spent.

The chief had been looking through the observation port in the upper part of the door. After a moment he slid the heavy metal battle shield across it. The compartment was still flooding, he announced. They needed to close the voice tubes. Henry joined the search for the key to the voice tube locker, but by now he was shivering violently and his thoughts were wandering.

"Must've swallowed too much salt water," he thought dazedly. Feeling weak and ineffectual, he wrapped himself in a blanket and curled up in one of the lower bunks in the battery room. Before long he stopped shaking, but he still didn't feel well; so he lay there and watched his shipmates pick up the dishes that had slid off the mess table and mop up the water that had spilled in from the control room.

## 13:57—Control Room.

How long had it taken to stop the flooding, Savvy wondered? Surely less than a minute, but he'd lost his stopwatch and could only guess at the time. He peered at a nearby depth gauge. It read fifty feet, which wasn't too bad, but the needle was rising and the deck was still slanted toward the bow.

Savvy glanced at the diving rudder controls. They were set for hard rise, just as he'd instructed. At the air manifold Chief Whitehead was still cycling compressed air into the ballast tanks. Everything was as it should be to bring them back to the surface, yet they were heading down instead of up. Why?

His unspoken question was answered a few seconds later, when a seaman thrust his head through the doorway to the battery room and yelled, "Water's coming into the torpedo room!"

How could *that* be? They had just closed the main induction valve, which should have halted flooding throughout the sub. Then the truth hit him. He and Grisham had closed the ventilator outlet here in the control room *first*. That had stopped the flooding, not the main valve. In fact, with the local valve shut, they had no direct way of determining the status of the main valve. However, if flooding was still going on in other parts of the sub, the main valve must be open.

The *S-Five* was evidently headed for the bottom and there was nothing they could do about it.

"Close watertight doors!" Savvy bawled.

The sub might survive hitting the bottom; but if water got into the battery compartment and the batteries failed, they'd have no light, no heat, no way to run the sub's motors or pumps, and they might as well be dead. Charlie Grisham had obviously reached the same conclusion; he was already at the forward bulkhead heaving on the battery room door. Savvy started over to help him, but before he'd taken a step the sub struck bottom. She rebounded once and then buried her nose in the sea floor.

# 3

# ON THE BOTTOM

"Oak and triple bronze encircled the heart of the man
who first committed a frail boat to the cruel sea."

—HORACE

WHEN THE *S-Five* was commissioned in the spring of 1920, the
U.S. Navy's submarine fleet was barely twenty years old. Although
the Navy Department had experimented with prototype subs before the turn of the century, it didn't commit itself formally to the
new era in sea power until April 11, 1900. On that day it spent
$150,000 to purchase a fifty-three-foot, seventy-five-ton subma-
rine called the *Holland VI* from its inventor, Irish immigrant John
Holland.

The Navy named its new submarine the U.S.S. *Holland*, which
must have pleased Mr. Holland; but for the next decade American
subs were christened more imaginatively after sea animals like the
*Shark* and venomous creatures like the *Viper*. In 1911 this colorful
system was replaced by a drab alpha-numeric nomenclature
(which is how the *S-Five* got its name). While making the various
classes of submarines easier to distinguish, the new system was
not very appealing. It lasted until 1931, when the old style of nam-
ing was reinstated.

The *Holland* was the first submarine capable of traveling long
distances (i.e., forty miles) underwater. It used a forty-five-

horsepower gasoline engine for propulsion on the surface and a battery-powered motor when submerged. This combination was used for more than a decade in American subs, even after it became obvious that gasoline was far too hazardous. In the enclosed space of a submarine's engine room gasoline fumes and air formed an explosive mixture. Even a small spark could set it off—and frequently did. Between 1900 and 1920 gasoline fires and explosions claimed the lives of more than thirty submariners around the world.

For years naval officers like Savvy Cooke's friend Chester Nimitz advocated the use of another power source. Finally in 1912 the Navy followed the French example and replaced gasoline engines with the safer and more efficient diesels, which didn't require complex ignition systems and didn't produce explosive fumes. The U.S.S. *Skipjack* (*SS-Twenty-four*) (commanded by Nimitz himself) was the first U.S. sub equipped for diesel propulsion. Unfortunately older boats continued to operate with the dangerous gasoline engines for many years, sometimes with tragic consequences.

The first gasoline related fatality in an American sub took place in 1902, when fire broke out in the engine room of the *Grampus* (Submarine *A-Three*) at dockside. A sailor was killed. As time passed, more accidents occurred. The worst involved the *Shark* (later known as Submarine *A-Seven*). Built in 1901 at the Crescent Shipyard in New York, the *Shark* spent her first seven years operating along the New England coast. In 1908, along with her sister ship, the *Porpoise,* she was loaded onto the deck of a coal transport and carried out to the Philippines, where both subs were put to work patrolling the entrance to Manila Bay. On July 24, 1917, shortly after leaving the dock, the *Shark* was jolted by an explosion, as gasoline fumes in her engine room ignited. Fire began to sweep through the boat. Under the command of her skipper, Lieutenant Junior Grade Arnold Marcus, her crew fought the blaze for nearly an hour. When it was clear that they couldn't extinguish it, Marcus ordered his men into waiting rescue boats, took the helm and tried to drive the *Shark* onto the beach to save her while his men were evacuated. He was the last to leave the sub and refused treatment for his burns until all of the other injured crewmen had received medical attention. He died the next day along with six of his men. In 1919 the destroyer U.S.S. *Marcus* was named in his honor.

Undersea technology advanced steadily during the first part of the twentieth century. Besides diving rudders, Simon Lake introduced the forerunner of movable periscopes, as well as the conning tower and central control room. A few years later supplemental oxygen tanks and chemical carbon dioxide absorbents helped to extend the amount of time submarines could remain underwater. But even with these improvements submarines failed to catch on as an important part of naval warfare, because they still had one crucial weakness: limited mobility.

The world's first military submarine was the *Turtle*. Designed and built in 1776 by David Bushnell, an engineer and student at Yale College, the *Turtle* was intended to break the British blockade of New York harbor by attaching mines to the blockading ships underwater. Although it failed in this endeavor, the *Turtle* did demonstrate a number of advanced features, such as air vents and ballast tanks.

In one respect, however, Bushnell's invention was hopelessly primitive: it moved through the water by means of *hand*-powered propellers. During the next century submarines became increasingly sophisticated, but their means of propulsion lagged far behind. In 1865, while steam-powered frigates and ironclads sped across the surface, subs like the Confederacy's *H.L. Hunley* still crept along underwater, like the *Turtle,* using muscle power.

Naturally the only targets for such pokey submersibles were stationary vessels like the ships blockading seaports. In fact, the submarine did make close naval blockade obsolete, just as Admiral George Dewey predicted decades earlier; but few people believed that subs would ever find a wider military use. Even the self-propelled torpedo, invented in 1868 by British engineer

Robert Whitehead and quickly adapted for submarine launching, didn't change military opinion. The problem with submarines wasn't their armament; it was their limited speed and range.

When internal combustion engines and electric motors were introduced around the turn of the century, submarines became more versatile; but even then they couldn't venture more than a few hundred miles from home port. When they did travel to remote parts of the world, they went as cargo, like the *Shark*, disassembled and lashed to the decks of large surface transports. Even these relatively modern subs couldn't keep up with steam-powered warships on the open sea; and so they were relegated to defensive roles in and around harbors and ports. The Congressional Act that appropriated funding for the S-Class submarines in 1916 actually described them as "coast submarines."

But in this case the description was *wrong*. For years American naval designers had dreamed of producing a "fleet" submarine, one that was capable of ranging along with surface warships far from home. The Germans had been the first to reach this goal with their *Unterseebooten* (soon to be known simply by the dreaded shorthand "U-Boats"). When the first U-Boat was launched in 1906, it was already an impressive achievement with a range of 2,000 miles and a top speed of nine knots submerged. On the eve of World War I, these capabilities had increased substantially, and by the war's end the Germans were producing 1,500 ton behemoths (the "UA" series) with ranges over 12,000 miles and top speeds exceeding fifteen knots. Ranging thousands of miles at sea, these killer subs ravaged British and allied shipping and even patrolled along the eastern coast of the United States.

Catching on belatedly, the British attempted to bridge the gap with their "K-Class" submarines, which used coal-fired steam engines to achieve high-speed and long range on the surface. With top speeds of up to twenty-four knots, the K-Class boats were definitely swift enough to compete with the U-boats, but they were plagued by accidents and the heat from their big steam boilers often made their engineering spaces uninhabitable. By 1920 all had been scrapped.

With their large size, powerful engines, and huge fuel capacity, the S-Class subs were the first American vessels to succeed as fleet submarines. The first S-Boat was begun in 1917 and launched in 1918. Although too late to influence the course of the war, it was a significant step for the American Navy, which finally had a submarine that could operate on the high seas. By 1920 S-Boats had established themselves as the backbone of the American submarine fleet, a position they would hold until the mid-1930s. Even after newer and more powerful subs had been developed, S-Boat squadrons played a significant part in the battle for the Pacific during World War II.[2]

Impressive as the S-Boats were in 1920, a number of questions about them remained unanswered. For instance, there were different *types* of S-Boat: the *S-One* was a "Holland type," the *S-Two* was a "Lake type," and the *S-Three* was a so-called "Government type."[3] At this stage in their development no one was sure which version would perform best or what problems might arise when the new subs were tested in the unforgiving laboratory of the sea. For the men who sailed in them, the S-Boats represented both a new age in undersea warfare and a calculated risk—as the crew of the *S-Five* would discover.

## WEDNESDAY, 14:05—ON THE BOTTOM.

The *S-Five* took about four minutes to reach the bottom. After she struck there was a long moment of silence in the control room, as everyone waited to see what the captain would do. Savvy's first act was to find out the status of his boat. According to the control room's gauges the submarine was upright and level in 180 feet of water. Luckily this part of the continental shelf consisted of relatively soft sand and mud, and the sub had struck at a shallow angle, actually skipping once before coming to rest. John Longstaff had

[2] This was partly because the newer subs used torpedoes with advanced magnetic proximity detonators that *didn't* work, while the S-Boats stuck with the reliable old contact detonators.

[3] Like the *S-One*, the *S-Four* and the *S-Five* were both Holland-type subs.

felt the impact as a slight shock in his knees. He'd watched the depth gauge drop a little, then rise past its previous reading as the *S-Five* settled onto the bottom. Many of the men on board didn't even feel that much.

Whether they noticed the impact or not, they could all be thankful for the soft landing, because at 180 feet the *S-Five's* pressure hull was more than halfway to its theoretical limit. Subjected to nearly 100 pounds per square inch of ocean pressure, it could easily have ruptured from a heavier jolt, as the *Titanic's* had a decade earlier. Like the *Titanic* the *S-Five* was made by riveting steel plates together. Riveted seams aren't very strong. They tend to split apart under stress, just as the seams on the *Titanic* did in 1912, when the liner struck an iceberg in the North Atlantic.

Welded seams are much sturdier than riveted seams. In fact, the welds are often stronger than the metal around them. But this technology wasn't available in 1920. It would be more than a decade before the first submarine with a welded pressure hull, the U.S.S. *Snapper*, was launched in 1937. During the coming hours the potential weakness of the *S-Five's* hull would become a persistent worry for Savvy.

As reports came in from other parts of the sub, Savvy began to get a better idea of the scope of the disaster. The worst flooding had apparently taken place in the control room and the torpedo room. That made sense. The *S-Five* had gone down by the head (nautical jargon for sinking bow first) and the water coming in through the induction system had simply flowed downhill. Eventually flooding would have become severe throughout the sub, as the forward compartments filled; but prompt action by the crew and some luck in the engine room had prevented a worse calamity. Savvy was convinced that without the efforts of Henry Love, John Smith, and the others, the *S-Five* would have flooded completely by the time she hit bottom.

Although the engine room and motor room had suffered less than the bow, they'd still taken in enough water to cause damage. For the moment both main drive motors were out of service, their wiring short-circuited, or "grounded," by the salt water that had saturated almost everything in the boat. The main lighting circuits were out too, but at least the emergency system was still intact for now. If it failed—Savvy repressed a shudder—they'd soon be fumbling around in pitch blackness, because the submarine's modest supply of flashlights and electric lanterns wouldn't last long as their sole source of light.

The news from the forward part of the boat was so discouraging that Savvy decided to find out firsthand how bad things were. Leaving Grisham in charge of the control room, he ducked through the forward bulkhead into the battery compartment. Almost a dozen men were gathered there. Many of them had been asleep in their bunks when the dive began, but they'd seen the flooding in the torpedo room and knew that something was wrong. Savvy stopped briefly to explain what had happened and to assure them that they were in no immediate danger. It was easy to sound confident. Thanks to Henry Love, who was curled up in one of the lower berths trying to get warm, only a small amount of water had gotten into the battery room, and most of had probably sprayed in from the control room.

A few minutes later, as Savvy peered through the small port-hole in the torpedo room's watertight door, he didn't feel at all complacent. Water had filled more than two-thirds of the compartment, partially covering the eye port, but he could see well enough to recognize a steady stream pouring in through the ventilator shaft, and when he put his ear to the door, he could hear a soft, steady rumbling.

So the main induction valve, the valve that Savvy and Grisham and Fox had worked so hard to close, was still at least partially open, and the flooding that had brought them to the bottom was still going on. It was the worst news Savvy had yet received.

When Savvy passed back through the battery room, he found the crew busily mopping up the water that had splashed in from the control room and putting the compartment back in order. The sight gave him a warm feeling. The men knew they were in deadly danger; but instead of panicking, they were sticking to their du-

ties, waiting to see what would come next. After all, they were submariners.


A WORLD WAR II SUBMARINE COMMANDER once remarked
that only individuals with "a certain psychological attitude" were
suited to the submarine service. If anything, he was understating
the case. In addition to mental stresses like claustrophobia,
crowding, and lack of privacy, early submariners had to endure
levels of physical discomfort that most people would find unbear-
able. Hot in summer, cold in winter, and incessantly damp from
condensation, subs were notorious for poor hygiene, minimal
fresh water, bad air . . . the list of inconveniences went on and on.
It's easy to see why the submarine service had to be strictly volun-
tary. It's not as easy to see why anyone would have joined.

There were some compensations to be sure. While on patrol
submarine crews ate better than sailors in the conventional Navy,
probably because food was one of the few luxuries the Navy could
provide on subs; and when they were in port, they moved ashore
and lived in relatively comfortable barracks. The money was good
too. Submariners were paid $5 per month more than surface
sailors; and ever since President Teddy Roosevelt's first submerged ride in 1905, they received a bonus of a dollar for each day
of diving. The bonuses were capped at $15 per month, but in 1920
twenty extra bucks month was real money that could increase a
sailor's income by 50 percent.

Taken altogether, however, it's unlikely that material benefits
alone made up for the drawbacks of the submarine service. There
had to be something else about it, something intangible.

Pride certainly played a role. To join the submarine service was
to become an adventurer into a new and unknown world, a world
of stealth and secrecy. Submarines could go where other ships
dared not, strike where other ships could not, and slip away unde-
tected to strike again. Here was power and prestige of a sort for
those willing to pay the price.

The pride of the undersea service had a personal dimension,

too, because everyone on a submarine from the captain down to the lowest enlisted rating had to master a great deal of sophisticated technology in order to do his job. There was no room on a sub for the old-fashioned *ordinary seaman,* qualified only to chip paint or pull on a rope's end. Submariners had to be smart and capable.

As subs became increasingly complex, the requirements for their crews became more demanding. In 1917, in recognition of the unique expertise required of submariners, a special training center was established at New London, Connecticut. The United States Naval Submarine School was an important step in the creation of an elite undersea corps with its own traditions and loyalty.

The informality aboard subs may have been a factor in their *esprit.* Unlike the surface Navy, with its emphasis on rank and protocol, the undersea service had a distinctively casual way of doing things. In the intensely practical environment of a submarine on patrol, uniforms, insignia of rank, and the ceremonies that went along with them became a waste of time. Fresh water for showers and laundry was often unavailable, so standards of personal appearance couldn't have a high priority either. People on subs tended to wear whatever was most practical. Savvy Cooke's usual shipboard attire consisted of a turtleneck sweater and khaki trousers. In a letter home one of his officers wrote, "You'd think he was on the way to milk the cows, if you saw him."

Living arrangements in subs contributed to the informality. Especially in the earliest boats, lack of space made it impossible to give the officers separate quarters. The close proximity led to a degree of familiarity between officers and enlisted men that would have been unthinkable in other branches of the tradition-conscious U.S. Navy.

Of all the ties that bound submariners together, however, danger was probably the strongest. The sea is notoriously unforgiving, but it reserves its harshest penalties for those who venture beneath its surface. A mistake that might be embarrassing or even humorous on a surface ship was often fatal—instantly fatal—in a submarine and not just for the sailor who made it, but for every one of his shipmates too. These risks were dramatically illustrated by the number of peacetime fatalities that occurred during the early years of the service.

Between 1900 and 1920 the world's navies lost sixteen submarines in non-combat accidents: an average of one sub every fifteen months! Most of these accidents were caused by collisions with other vessels or mistakes involving open hatches or valves. Even today subs are more vulnerable than surface ships; they're more fragile and have little or no built-in buoyancy. When something goes wrong, they tend to go down quickly; and they usually take all hands with them, because, once the sea begins pouring in through a breach in the hull or an open hatch, there's little chance for anyone inside a sub to escape. More than 400 sailors died in those sixteen accidents. At a time when submarines seldom carried more than twenty or thirty men, such figures leave little doubt about the chances for survival then.

Most of the men who rode the *S-Five* to the bottom on that sunny fall day in 1920 were unaware of these grim statistics, but many of them had heard stories about American losses. Sixty-two of the 400 men who'd died during the previous two decades had been U.S. sailors.

Three years earlier, for example, on December 17, 1917 during exercises off Port Loma, California, U.S.S. *F-One* collided with her sister ship, the *F-Three*. With her port side torn wide open the *F-One* sank in *ten seconds,* taking nineteen of her twenty-two crewmen with her.

The problems were by no means confined to the American navy. While serving on British subs during the war, both Savvy and Fred Whitehead had heard terrible stories. While training off the Isle of Wight in March 1904, submarine H.M.S. *A1* was struck by the steamship *Berwick Castle*. Believing that she'd hit a stray buoy or derelict practice torpedo, the *Castle* proceeded on her way. There was no one to dispute her assumption, because the sub and all her crew had disappeared. Five years later, British submarine H.M.S. *C11* sank with all but one of her crew after a collision in the English Channel.

All of these accidents were so abrupt and so devastating that the men involved in them probably drowned immediately. On the other hand, newer subs were equipped with strong internal bulkheads and watertight doors. Given a few seconds to respond, the crew of a wounded submarine might find temporary refuge in a sealed compartment. After that, of course, if they weren't rescued, they risked an even crueler fate, waiting helplessly on the bottom for their air to run out or the hull to collapse.

Had men actually died like that? No one in the *S-Five* knew for sure, but some of them had heard a horrific tale about an American sub called the *F-Four.* Originally named the *Skate,* the *F-Four* was launched in Seattle on June 6, 1912. After serving for two years along the West Coast, she was tied onto the deck of a freighter and hauled out to Hawaii: a move that her young crewmen must have considered a lucky break because the *Skate* was one of only four subs posted to the islands. Three years later, however, their luck ran out. On March 25, 1915, during a submerged run barely a mile and a half off Honolulu, the *Skate* sank. Investigators later concluded that salt water seeping into her battery well had caused her to lose power.

She came to rest in 300 feet of water with her pressure hull miraculously intact. When she failed to report on schedule, an alarm was raised. Within a short time searchers had followed a telltale oil slick and rising bubbles to locate her. Twenty-four hours of heroic effort by Navy divers and tugs with grappling cables failed to raise her. Finally, when it was clear that her crew could not have survived, the rescue effort was called off.

Five months later the *F-Four* was dragged into shallow water and brought to the surface using inflatable pontoons. At the time this was considered an impressive engineering feat, but it came far too late for the men trapped inside her. Details of what was found when the *Skate* was opened weren't widely published, but word went around that fifteen of her crew had taken refuge in the engine room after she hit bottom. The ensuing hours must have been dreadful indeed for those sailors. Without power it would have been dark down there and wet and cold, and they could only have waited helplessly, as the cables scraped and slipped along the hull and the sub lurched and rolled to no avail.

The *F-Four* wasn't the only submarine to meet a lingering end. Although none of the *S-Fives* had heard of it, there was another story, about a Japanese sub. In the last year of their 1905 war with Russia, the Imperial Japanese Navy had bought five Holland-type boats from the Electric Boat Company, as well as blueprints for a smaller version of the same sub. After much time and effort they built and launched two of these, which they named with characteristic economy *Boat #6* and *Boat #7*. After the war these seven boats formed the first Japanese submarine squadron.

On April 15, 1910, *Boat #6* was practicing a submerged run using a snorkel, a large tube extending above the surface to draw in air and expel engine exhaust. To prevent flooding, the snorkel was equipped with a flapper valve activated by a steel chain, but on that day the chain broke, allowing tons of water to enter through the snorkel. *Boat #6* sank immediately. She came to rest in shallow water, but not shallow enough for the crew to escape. After all efforts had failed, the men apparently sat down at their posts and calmly prepared to die. Their captain used the dim glow from the conning tower porthole to write a detailed report of the accident. He concluded by commending his crew and asking the Japanese government to provide for their families.

Whether they had heard any of these stories or not, the men in the *S-Five* knew that they were in grave danger, and no one knew it better than their skipper. As Savvy retraced his steps to the control room, he reviewed their situation. It wasn't an encouraging picture. The *S-Five* was due to arrive in Baltimore Thursday evening or Friday morning, but it was unlikely that anyone would notice her absence—or at least make an issue of it—until midday on Friday, when the opening ceremony for the recruiting drive was scheduled to take place. That was nearly two days in the future.

Even after they were missed, there was little likelihood that anyone would find them. The search techniques, such as "active

SONAR,"[4] that are taken for granted today simply didn't exist in 1920. Given a general notion of where a sub had gone down, surface ships could listen for telltale sounds using the primitive hydrophones of the day. With a more exact idea of a sub's location, they could drag for her with grappling hooks or send down hardhat divers to search for her, but all of these methods were unreliable, time-consuming, and, in the case of divers, hazardous.

Shortly before the war, "telephone buoys" had been developed to aid in the location of sunken submarines. Mounted on the outside of the pressure hull, so that they could be released from the inside, these buoys were designed to rise to the surface and float, tethered by cables that contained telephone lines. If a rescue vessel found such a buoy, the telephone cable permitted communication with the submarine's crew and the tether guided divers down to the wreck. During World War I these buoys were discontinued, because the Navy feared that accidental deployment might reveal submarines to enemy warships. Buoy or no buoy, in the part of the ocean where the *S-Five* had gone down there wasn't much ship traffic. Besides, Savvy's last-minute course change insured that no one would know where to look for them.

As for escaping from the *S-Five* where she lay on the ocean floor, this was out of the question. It was only 160 feet from the conning tower hatch to the surface, little more than half the length of a football field, but that distance posed an insurmountable obstacle. At a depth of 160 feet seawater exerts almost five times the normal atmospheric pressure of fifteen pounds per square inch. Applied over the area of the conning tower hatch, this amounted to a pressure difference of nearly fifty tons. In effect, water pressure had sealed the crew inside the *S-Five* as tightly as if her hatches had been welded shut. Even if divers had been able to reach her, they wouldn't have been able to pry the hatches open against that kind of resistance. During salvage oper-

---

[4] SONAR, the acronym for "SOund NAvigation & Ranging," is underwater echo-location, the source of the "pinging" noises so familiar from submarine movies.

ations divers customarily blasted hatches open with explosives, but that wasn't feasible with men inside.

During tours of the sub, it was customary to tell visitors that hatches were the only way in or out of a sub, but Savvy knew that wasn't strictly true. Theoretically the torpedo tubes could serve as emergency exits, but the method had significant limitations. In order to prevent accidental flooding, torpedo tubes were equipped with interlocks, so that their outer doors could be opened only when the inner doors had been locked shut and the tubes filled with water. Nevertheless, in 1910 a Navy officer named Kenneth Whiting decided to test whether a torpedo tube could function as an escape route. At the time Whiting was the commanding officer of the sixty-three-foot submarine *Porpoise,* which was stationed in the Philippines. On the morning of April 15, 1901, the *Porpoise* leveled off in the shallow waters of Manila Bay and Ensign Whiting squeezed into one of the sub's eighteen-inch torpedo tubes. Hanging on to a metal brace on the outer door while the tube flooded, Whiting waited until the door opened, squirmed out of the tube and swam to the surface. In all his escape took seventy-seven seconds.

Savvy was aware of Whiting's daring experiment. He knew also about an early German submarine, the *U-Three,* whose crew had escaped through the torpedo tubes when their boat foundered in 1911. But he still didn't consider the *S-Five*'s torpedo tubes to be a realistic escape route. Whiting had emerged from the *Porpoise* into the warm sunlit water of Manila Bay at a depth of only twenty feet. The German sub had gone down in shallow water. But the *S-Five* lay in water that was nearly ten times deeper. It was dark down there and cold, only a few degrees above freezing. Anyone who managed to claw his way out of a torpedo tube into the frigid blackness outside the *S-Five*'s hull would be dead long before he could reach the surface.

Like most submariners, Savvy had encountered people who couldn't understand this. "Say it's only a hundred feet," they would exclaim, "Why, I can hold my breath and swim that far!" But, as any diver could have told them, ascending from a hundred feet is altogether different from swimming the same stretch along the surface. At a depth of thirty feet the external pressure on a diver's body is twice what it is at the surface, at sixty feet it's three times as much and so forth. Body tissues are composed mainly of water and are therefore incompressible, but body *cavities* are not. Lungs, stomach, sinuses, middle ear, all suffer compressive effects as the depth increases.

For example, unequal pressures between the inner and outer ear can cause severe pain and even rupture the eardrum. In other parts of the body the same kind of pressure imbalance can create more serious effects. Below a depth of about fifty feet the chest wall can no longer flex inward enough to equalize internal and external pressures. The resulting imbalance draws excess blood into the chest cavity, straining the heart and causing lung congestion or even hemorrhage. Compression makes the human body less buoyant: instead of floating toward the surface, a diver coming up from the depths must work against gravity.

The world record for free diving—descending and ascending on a single breath of air—reached 180 feet (the depth at which the *S-Five* lay) only in the mid-1960s, and that was accomplished by highly trained athletes competing under carefully controlled conditions. For untrained sailors struggling to escape from a submarine under extremely adverse conditions, the odds against success would be literally overwhelming.

Of course, Savvy and his shipmates couldn't have known these facts, but their instincts, combined with the bitter history of submarine accidents, told them that they had little hope of escaping. Prior to 1920 *not one* sailor had survived a deep-water sinking like theirs. A decade later Charles "Swede" Momsen would begin the experiments leading to his famous rescue chamber and the "Momsen Lung," which enabled submariners to breathe compressed air as they swam to safety. His pioneering work would be dramatically vindicated in 1939, when he rescued thirty-three sailors from the submarine *Squalus* after it sank in forty fathoms off Portsmouth.

But for Savvy Cooke and his men, Lieutenant Momsen's

achievements were part of the unknowable future. Unlike the crew of the *Squalus*, they had little hope of being found; and in the unlikely event that someone did stumble across them, there was even less likelihood that they could be rescued. Their only chance for survival was to get the *S-Five* back to the surface themselves before their air supply ran out.

And the clock was already ticking.

# 4

# STRATEGIES

"Courage is resistance to fear . . . not absence of fear."
—MARK TWAIN

WEDNESDAY, 14:15—CONTROL ROOM.

When Savvy returned from his inspection of the torpedo room, Chief Electrician Ramon Otto was already hard at work on the electrical systems. A sturdy, dark-haired man from the town of Brant Rock just outside Boston, Otto was an expert submariner. After joining the Navy in 1913 he'd served on a number of subs, including one of Savvy Cooke's former commands. Otto was no stranger to the hazards of the undersea service. His face and arms still bore the dark tracery of burns he'd suffered in a previous shipboard accident.

Assisting Otto was a second class electrician named Walter Nelson. "Nels," as his friends called him, was another Massachusetts native, hailing from Methuen, a town just below the New Hampshire border. During the crash dive he'd been stationed with Otto at the main switchboard and had participated in the frantic effort to maintain power. Now he was helping the Chief to put things right.

Otto had decided to restore the *S-Five*'s main lighting system first, because the auxiliary system was so weak. Besides making things look unnecessarily gloomy, the dim illumination made gauges hard to read and hampered repair work. Of the sub's two main lighting circuits, one was unsalvageable; but the other was intact, except for a small short circuit in one of the torpedo indicator circuits. This "partial ground" was allowing current from the entire system to drain away uselessly. As Otto knew very well, the textbook solution for such a problem was to pull the fuse for the defective section and cut it off from the rest of the system, but that particular fuse was in a hard-to-reach spot. Rather than waste time trying to get to it, Otto decided to take a shortcut. He sent Nelson into the battery room with a screwdriver. When the electrician had exposed the wires leading to the torpedo light, Otto fed current into the system again and yelled, "Okay!" Nelson bridged his screwdriver across the wires, producing a large blue spark and a loud *pop*. The inaccessible feeder fuse promptly blew, and with the current drain eliminated, the overhead lights flickered and brightened.

Savvy was making his way aft from the torpedo room, when the lights came up. He breathed a sigh of relief. The improved lighting would make their work easier and improve morale too. His next priority was to close the main induction valve once and for all. As soon as he reached the control room, he ordered Percy Fox to assemble a work party of the strongest sailors he could find. Within minutes the husky chief petty officer and several other big men were hard at work, once again using the huge spanner for leverage. They managed to turn the wheel a surprising amount; but, when they gave up at last and stood, hands on knees, panting from their efforts, no one could say whether they'd succeeded or not.

The main induction valve consisted of a circular "gate" that moved up or down inside the pipe to open or close it. This gate was connected by a long threaded shaft to the overhead control wheel, which also moved up or down as the valve operated. The distance that the hand wheel descended into the control room as it turned was therefore an indication of the valve's status, but it wasn't precise enough. Savvy had to send Grisham forward to the torpedo room in order to observe the leak directly. When the exec returned a few minutes later, Savvy could tell from his expression that it hadn't been stopped.

Regretfully he shelved that issue for the moment. Time was precious and they couldn't afford to squander it in a vain attempt to close the main induction valve, no matter how desirable that might be. Turning to Ramon Otto he asked a question that had been nagging at him since they'd hit the bottom.

How were the drive motors?"

According to Otto the port drive motor was irreparably damaged; an overload relay had blown inside its motor housing. But the starboard motor was operational. Savvy accepted the chief electrician's assessment thoughtfully; their situation wasn't as bad as he'd feared. Ordinarily a single drive motor would have more than enough power to raise the sub. Whether it would suffice now depended on two critical questions.

First, how much extra weight had been added to the sub by the flooding? From what Savvy had seen, the torpedo room held about forty-five tons of sea water. The bilges in the control room probably contained another fifteen tons, and the engine room and motor room bilges about half that much. So altogether the S-Five was about seventy-five tons—or 10 percent—heavier than usual.

Second, how much additional buoyancy could they get from the ballast tanks to overcome that extra weight? When Savvy stopped at the air manifold on his way back from the bow, Chief Whitehead speculated that the forward ballast tanks might still contain a substantial amount of water. The S-Five had been tilted sharply forward during the dive, and the Kingston valves were at the rear of the tanks. Now that the sub was level again, it should be possible to blow that water out. Unfortunately the ballast tanks weren't equipped with gauges, so there was no way to estimate how much "leftover buoyancy" there might be. The only way to find out was to blow the tanks and see what happened.

That is, if they had enough compressed air to do it. They'd used a great deal of air on the way down; and once their original supply was gone, that was the end of it, because the air compressors weren't running either.

Savvy walked back to the forward end of the control room and asked for a status report. To his relief, Whitehead responded that two of the three air banks were full. Fred had already sent men forward and aft to close the air vents on the ballast tanks. "Captain," he said, "we're ready to blow!"

Savvy looked at the chronometer on the control room bulkhead. It read 14:25. They'd been on the bottom almost thirty minutes and so far they'd been relatively lucky: the sub's hull was intact and they still had light, air, and power; but there was no guarantee how long any of these would last. Virtually everything in the sub had been drenched with seawater. Every minute that passed made it more likely that a vital piece of equipment would fail. Every minute allowed additional flooding in the torpedo room. It was time to make a concerted effort to raise the sub, before their predicament grew much worse. After all, *if* the batteries held up, *if* their single drive motor had enough power, *if* enough water could be blown out of the ballast tanks, and *if* the sub wasn't stuck too deep in the mud, they might be able to reach the surface.

Because the *S-Five* had plowed head-on into the bottom, Savvy decided to back her out. He began issuing orders: "Rudders to hard rise. Blow safety and forward tanks. Blow midships tanks. Starboard motor, *back* 1800 amps."

The control room began to buzz with activity, acquiring for the moment a pleasant air of normalcy. Percy Fox adjusted the diving rudders, which had to be reversed since the sub was backing. At the switchboard Chief Otto routed current into the starboard motor circuit, while at the air manifold Fred Whitehead began to bleed compressed air into the ballast tanks. The squeal of expanding air mingled eerily with the creak of the hull and the low-pitched thrum of the propeller. The *S-Five* shifted and seemed to straighten. Throughout the sub men waited tensely for the soft lurch that would tell them she had lifted off the bottom. Those who were near depth gauges stared at them as though sheer willpower could make the readings change.

But they didn't. At first the sub merely quivered and stayed where she was. Then, to the consternation of everyone, she began to roll over onto her port side. Savvy realized immediately that the starboard ballast tanks were emptying too fast and unbalancing the sub. Once again the Kingston valves were at fault!

"Stop blowing," he barked. "Close starboard Kingstons!"

Electricians Frank Peters and Walter Nelson were nearest to the Kingstons. Leaving their posts at once they scrambled to the rear of the control room and unlocked the levers, only to discover how hard it would be to carry out the captain's order. As the *S-Five* tilted onto her port side, the starboard controls were being lifted out of reach! By straddling between the deck and the wall of the galley, Peters and Nelson worked their way high enough to release the hand brakes at the top of the levers; but the valves seemed even stickier than usual, and both men wound up dangling in the air, heaving and jerking on the levers like fish on a line.

By this time Charlie Grisham and several other crewmen had arrived to help. One by one the valves were closed. As the water level in the ballast tanks evened out, the sub shuddered to a halt. At the air manifold, Fred Whitehead drew a shaky breath. The *S-Five* had rolled nearly thirty degrees to port. Any further, and the water sloshing toward that side in the ballast tanks might have turned her completely over. And that, Fred concluded grimly, would have done for them.

They weren't out of danger yet. Fred's thoughts were interrupted by a shout.

"She's coming back!" Percy Fox yelled.

His warning came too late. Lacking any way of gauging their efforts, Nelson and the others had overcompensated. Now the imbalance was on the other side. As the submarine began to right herself, it became obvious that she was moving too fast. The port Kingstons would have to be adjusted now, but by the time they'd been unlocked and manhandled into submission, the sub had gone past vertical and onto her starboard side. For a moment she quivered there, poised between disaster and recovery, and then started back again.

And so it went. The shifting buoyancies rocked the *S-Five* violently from side to side, while the starboard propeller dragged her lurching and bumping across the sea floor, subjecting the hull to a terrible battering. Aware that the gyrations might flip the sub onto her side and crush the conning tower, or even roll her over completely, the men at the Kingstons worked like demons, scrambling to maintain their balance on the slippery, shifting surfaces, as they pushed and pulled on the levers. One moment they would have to haul almost straight up to close a valve and the next almost straight down as the sub swung to the other side. All the while they could hear loud grinding and crashing sounds coming from beneath the boat. For them and for the rest of the crew, hanging on wherever they could, the suspense was horrible. Would the sub pull herself free and head for the surface? Or would the hull, already subjected to forces beyond anything its designers had intended, give in to the strain and rupture?

At the electrical panel a main circuit breaker tripped, cutting off current to the drive motor. Otto slapped it back in place. A few seconds later the breaker tripped again, and yet again. The third time it burst into flames and Otto threw up his hands in disgust. The propeller spun to a stop. Gradually the men at the Kingstons brought the oscillations under control, and as the ballast tanks finally emptied, the *S-Five* came back to an even keel. It was clear that the buoyancy hadn't increased enough to lift her. Without even a single drive motor to propel her toward the surface, she settled back into the mud.

"I'd say we earned our dollar for this dive, Nels!" Frank Peters panted, as he and Nelson replaced the locking bars on the control levers. He referred to the modest bonus pay that submariners received for each day of diving. When the Kingstons had been secured, Frank threaded his way between recumbent sailors, heading back toward the radio shack.

With both of the sub's forward compartments sealed off, the

control room had become quite congested. A half dozen men had retreated up the ladder into the conning tower, which helped a little. Nevertheless, Frank wasn't at all surprised to find that two crewmen had taken refuge in the radio shack. One of them was perched on top of his equipment rack, the other had tucked himself underneath it.

The unexpected call to man the Kingstons had interrupted Frank while he was attempting to send out a distress signal. Although he knew that the sub's radio was unlikely to make contact at this depth, it was surely worth a try.

"As long as you're here," he suggested to his visitors, "you can give me a hand."

Seawater had soaked Frank's radio apparatus and he needed help keeping wires and other components apart so that they wouldn't short circuit. Replacement fuses were getting hard to find. A few minutes later, while the sailors gingerly separated his leads, Frank sent out a signal using the old-fashioned spark system that had served amateur radio operators for more than a decade. After tapping out a series of S.O.S. calls, he hunched over the crystal receiver, cupping the headset to his ears and straining to hear a response; but, although he methodically tuned the vernier from one end of the scale to the other, he heard only faint static, and the meters showed no evidence of a signal.

The attempt came to an abrupt end, when one of his helpers inadvertently touched a metal bucket lying beneath the bench. As current coursed through the sailor's body, his muscles jerked and he uttered a yelp of pained surprise. Rolling out from under the bench, he glared at his friend, who was doubled up with laughter. "It ain't funny!" he said, but Peters was grinning, too. Soon all three of them were sharing the joke, but the reality of their situation wasn't amusing. If Peters couldn't use the radio to inform the outside world of what had happened to them, the men of the S-Five would remain on their own.

At the other end of the control room, Savvy Cooke was coming to an equally depressing conclusion. With her drive motors permanently out of commission, his sub was little more than an inert hulk. The only way to get her to the surface now was to make her buoyant enough to float, and that meant dealing with the flooded torpedo room. So far their attempts to close the main induction valve had failed. Savvy saw no reason to continue that effort; but if they couldn't stop the leak, there was only one other option: they'd have to remove the water faster than it was coming in.

Savvy called Charlie Grisham over to confer. A few minutes later Charlie walked back into the engine room and ordered Chief Hutson to connect the *S-Five*'s high-pressure pump to the torpedo-room bilges. Recruiting John Smith and Walter Nelson, who were relaxing on a nearby bale of rags, Hutson led them back into the motor room, where the main pumps were located.

To many people the interior of a World War I submarine resembles nothing so much as a plumber's nightmare: a bewildering web of reservoirs, pipes, pumps, gauges, and valves filling nearly every available space, with human conveniences like bunks and lockers squeezed in wherever possible. Visitors often asked why the sub needed such extravagant piping. The answer was simple: *buoyancy control.* In order for a submarine to remain level underwater, its weight had to be balanced precisely. This was accomplished by pumping fluids like fuel, water, and air from place to place through the sub's rigid structure. It was important. Even small imbalances in weight or buoyancy could produce dramatic results (as the *S-Five* had just demonstrated). To keep the network of piping as simple as possible, its components were designed to be interchangeable, so that the same devices could be used for different purposes.

The high-pressure pump was one of these interchangeable devices. Located in the motor room, it was a powerful, three-stage centrifugal pump capable of developing a pressure head of over 100 pounds per square inch. This was more than enough force to drive water out of the sub even at a depth of 180 feet and with its 300-gallon-per-minute capacity, there was even a chance that the pump could empty the flooded torpedo room in spite of the leak.

It took some time for the engineers to make the necessary connections: from the pump in the motor room through the sub's central drainage duct to the bilge system, but Grisham felt confident that their efforts would pay off. As the sub's safety officer he'd tested that pump only a few days before the sinking and it had worked flawlessly. Once it was up and running, he predicted cheerfully, "We'll be merrily on our way up to the surface!"

### 15:00—Motor Room.

Charlie Grisham would have been considerably less cheerful had he known what was going on in the stern at that moment. Not long after Hutson and his men went back to start the high-pressure pump, John Smith stuck his head into the engine room and asked Chief Bender to lay aft and give them a hand. As Bender passed through the doorway into the motor room, he heard the high-pressure pump purring steadily and assumed it was working fine. Then he saw water spurting across the deck. The pump's outlet gasket had failed and seawater was spewing into the room faster than it was being pumped into the sea!

Bender told Hutson to shut the pump down while he called the control room by voice tube. When he informed Savvy of the failure, the Captain's response was predictable: *Fix it!*

Half an hour later, after trying every trick he knew, Bender had to admit defeat. No one had been able to find a replacement gasket and nothing else seemed adequate to use as a substitute. Reluctantly he called the control room to convey the bad news.

The loss of the high-pressure pump was a hard blow. With it they might have gotten back to the surface within an hour or two, just as Grisham had predicted. Without it they would have to rely on the sub's *low*-pressure pump, which was rated at only thirty-five gallons per minute. That was bad enough, but there was worse to come. When the engineers activated the low-pressure pump, the circuit breaker in its motor control tripped repeatedly. Ramon Otto became so frustrated that he stalked back to the motor room and stuffed rags into the breaker to hold it closed, but the pump still wouldn't develop effective suction. The combination of the crippled electrical system and the high external water pressure was simply too much for it.

It would be impossible to overstate how perilous their situation had become at this point. In an environment where a *single* accident was often deadly, the *S-Five* had suffered one major malfunction after another. Now that the two main pumps had failed, their only remaining device for moving water was the *regulating pump,* a small, low-capacity device located in the control room and normally used to adjust the sub's trim.

Ignoring his conviction that the regulating pump would accomplish nothing, Savvy ordered Grisham to connect it to the torpedo room. To no one's surprise, it stalled at once, overcome by the eighty-five pounds per square inch of sea pressure at its outlet. Now all three pumps had failed!

It was now that Savvy demonstrated how he'd acquired his nickname. In addition to the bilge drains, which opened beneath the deck, the *S-Five* had an entirely separate air salvage system with openings near the *top* of each compartment. This system was designed so that divers could inject compressed air into a flooded submarine in order to raise her, but Savvy had thought of a different use for it.

He ordered the crew to spread through the boat, closing all the salvage outlets. When they had finished, the only compartment with an open salvage line was the inaccessible torpedo room. Next Savvy ordered Fred Whitehead to feed compressed air into the salvage system until the pressure had reached 100 pounds per square inch. This pressure would be transmitted through the salvage system directly to the water in the torpedo room. If Savvy was right, the additional force would enable the regulating pump to overcome the outside water pressure. Once again everyone waited.

For many of the crew, waiting had become the hardest part of their ordeal. With the sub dead in the water, most of them had no duties to perform and nothing to distract them from what might lie ahead. Some of the crew were convinced they were going to die; others thought they might live. As the hours dragged by, even the most experienced sailors vacillated between hope and despair, but their uncertainty was minor compared to the dread felt by the novice crewmen, whose imaginations found something new to fear in every unexpected bump.

Chief Bender didn't realize how hard some of them were taking it, until he saw tears glistening in the eyes of one of his junior firemen. The Chief shook his head; sometimes he forgot just how young these kids were. Most of them were still teenagers or barely out of their teens. In some ways, he had to admit, that was better, because the handful of older men who'd left wives and families at home were suffering the most.

### 15:00—Control Room.

Charlie Grisham was worried about his wife, Mary. As far as he could tell, she was reconciled to the life of a Navy wife, with its long absences and uncertainty; but he often wondered how she was handling the additional strain of the submarine service. He was grateful that Portsmouth was a Navy town, so she had support from other Navy wives, including women whose husbands were in subs.

But what would happen, Charlie wondered, if worse came to worst, and he and his shipmates didn't make it back this time? In spite of himself, he imagined the scene: Mary answering the door, her hair done up in the scarf she wore when she was cleaning. According to Navy tradition there'd be two people on the doorstep, one a senior officer from the base and the other probably a chaplain. Charlie could picture Mary's expression, the little frown she got when she was worried growing deeper as the implications of the visit became clearer. And then . . .

There was no point torturing himself about it now. Charlie focused his attention on the regulating pump, willing it to keep running.

On the other side of the control room Ramon Otto was trying to repair the second lighting circuit. Running one system without a backup made him nervous, and they could use the extra illumination for the work they were doing. Otto's eyes were burning from the strain of trying to read the voltage meter's scale in the dim light. With a sigh he put down the instrument, closed his eyes, and kneaded them gently.

While he waited for his eyes to recover, Otto's thoughts drifted. He was agonizing about insurance. Several weeks before the *S-Five* left Boston he'd applied for a new government insurance policy. With a family on the way, he and his wife Maud had decided it would be smart to get additional coverage. But the *S-Five* had sailed before he'd gotten a response, so he didn't know if the application had been approved. Maud was a strong, resourceful woman—it was one of the things he loved about her—but the thought of her without that extra protection in case something happened to him was a constant heartache.

He remembered how hard it had been for her when he'd been hurt. Lying in the hospital, wracked with pain, drifting in and out of consciousness, Otto had retained little sense of time. It must have seemed like centuries to poor Maud, but she'd been there for him, always at his side when he opened his eyes, smiling bravely and telling him that things would turn out fine.

Things *had* turned out fine. He'd survived and gone back to work. A year ago, when he'd been promoted to chief, he and Maud had put a down payment on a home in Brant Rock, north of Boston, a lovely old house with a view of the ocean. It had seemed like the right thing to do at the time, but now he wasn't so sure. If only that damned policy had been approved!

Savvy Cooke could console himself with the knowledge that his family was secure. Temple and Anne were in Arkansas, living with his parents and his sister, Cornelia, on the farm outside Fort Smith. His brothers John and Stephen were in the Navy, John as a submarine officer on the west coast and Stephen as a midshipman at Annapolis. His youngest brother, William, had married and was working for the railroad in Kansas, and sister Helen had also settled down back in Fort Smith. Doubtless they'd all miss him, especially the kids, if he didn't survive; but he hoped that eventually they'd understand why he was here.

## 15:00—Steering Platform.

George Bill looked around the steering platform at the huddled forms of his shipmates. It had been an eventful hour since the ill-starred crash dive. When the sub had first driven her nose into the bottom, Bill had realized at once that his usefulness as a helmsman had ended. Nevertheless, he'd stayed at his post on the steering platform, if for no other reason than to keep out of the way of Chief Otto and his men down in the control room. Five other crewmen had climbed up into the conning tower to join him, most likely for the same reason.

It was cold on the steering platform and a steady rain of condensation had dripped on their heads and shoulders, until Bill dug out a couple of raincoats that were stored there for the bridge watch. He was just spreading the slickers overhead, when the sub began rocking violently from side to side. The men on the steering platform scrambled to support themselves. It was obvious that the Captain had decided to blow the ballast tanks, but something must have gone wrong.

"It's those goddamn Kingstons," one of the engineers had grumbled, but Bill had been too busy hanging on to analyze possible causes. He had a momentary image of the sub flipping on her side and smashing the conning tower. It wouldn't take much to spring these hull plates, he thought, looking doubtfully at the nearest seam. What a fragile barrier it was to withstand the crushing ocean pressures outside.

But the *S-Five* didn't flip over and the hull didn't rupture. Eventually the rocking subsided. The men in the conning tower were just beginning to relax, when one of the youngest sailors lost control. Jumping up he began scrabbling at the upper hatch, the one leading to the bridge. There was no chance that he could open it, even if he knew how, not with all that pressure on the other side; but there was a definite risk that his panic could spread to other susceptible crewmembers. It took Bill and his mates several minutes to calm the youngster down. Then they began looking for ways to keep his spirits up, as well as their own.

"How about singing?" someone suggested. It was a good idea. These were the days before commercial radio,[5] when even gramophones were a novelty, and people were accustomed to making their own music. Many in the crew could play instruments and nearly everyone knew the words to popular songs like "Alexander's Ragtime Band."

The problem with singing, another sailor pointed out, was that it might drown out orders from the control room. He was right, so they found quieter things to do. A pair of dice materialized from somewhere and an impromptu game of craps sprang up. The other men propped themselves against the walls and talked.

Mostly they stuck to the usual topics of home, family, girls, but inevitably the conversation turned to baseball, which had already become a national obsession.[6] The World Series was about to start, pitting the Brooklyn Dodgers against the Cleveland Indians, and Fred Whitehead was taking all odds that his beloved "Bums" would win the pennant this year.

They talked about the sinking too. Nearly everyone had an opinion about what had happened, and about their chances, but in spite of the grim odds, most of them preferred to make fun of their situation. The sub's yeoman made everyone laugh by complaining that the flooding had destroyed his typewriter before he'd completed the daily log.

"I don't mind hitting the bottom," one of the sailors confided, then grinned and added, "as long as we come to the top again!"

There was serious talk as well. The helmsman who'd stood the

<hr />

[5] The country's first commercial radio station, KDKA Pittsburgh, would begin broadcasting in November 1920.

[6] Other professional sports were still in their infancy: the National Football League had just begun its first season in 1920, while the four-team National Hockey League was only in its third season.

morning watch admitted that he hated the thought of "dying in a trap" like this, but he went on to say that today's experience had taught him new respect for the German U-Boat crews he'd fought during the war. All of those German sailors deserved medals for bravery, he said. No one contradicted him.

As he listened to the other sailors, George Bill was struck by how calm they all seemed—with the exception of that one young fellow. Bill wasn't as fearful as he'd expected to be either. Instead, he felt an indescribable confidence that the captain would somehow pull them through; He wasn't the only one to feel this. As the disaster progressed and their chances of survival dwindled, most of the *S-Fives* looked to their commanding officer for courage and hope.

As for Savvy Cooke, if he ever knew fear or doubt during those perilous hours, it never showed. Calm, focused, outwardly confident, he was always ready with a kind word or a quiet joke to boost morale. It was as though he embodied the words inscribed on the medallion around his neck, the one given to him by his father. *Tu ne cede malis,* it read: "Never yield to misfortune."

# 5

## SAVVY

"To lead is to foresee."

—CHARLES M. COOKE

IN 1920 Savvy Cooke was thirty-three years old. Considering the hardscrabble circumstances of his childhood, he would probably have described his time in the Navy as the *best* fourteen years of his life. He was born Charles Maynard Cooke Junior on December 19, 1886, in Fort Smith, Arkansas—a small, but bustling military town on the banks of the Arkansas River. He came "of good stock," as the saying goes. On his mother's side he was related to Rear Admiral Stephen Bleecker Luce, founder of the Naval War College, as well as Henry Robinson Luce, founder of the Time-Life publishing empire.

Like many frontier towns in the years after the Civil War, Fort Smith was ripe with opportunity, but success eluded Savvy's father. An intelligent and ambitious man, Charles Senior had married well and at first seemed destined for great things. He was Fort Smith's city attorney for several years and served a term as the city's mayor; but he declined a second term for financial reasons and afterwards pursued a series of unprofitable and increasingly desperate business ventures. At length he fell into a rut of failure, frustration, and alcoholism from which he never recovered.

During Savvy's childhood the family lived on a small farm several miles outside Fort Smith, where they eked out an impoverished existence. When Savvy and his older brother, John, weren't in school, they helped to support their mother and four younger siblings by working odd jobs around the town. In later years Savvy wrote a poem about life on the farm. The tone is light-hearted, but between the lines, it's easy to discern harsh memories.

> *Down on the farm 'bout half past four*
> *I slip on my pants and sneak out of the door;*
> *Out of the yard I run like the dickens*
> *To milk 10 cows and feed the chickens,*
> *Clean out the barn, curry Nancy and Jiggs,*
> *Separate the cream and slop the pigs,*
> *Work 2 hours and then eat like a Turk,*
> *And, by heck, I'm ready for a full day's work!*

As a result of such hardships, Savvy became accustomed at an early age to taking on responsibility. In school it became obvious that he was intellectually gifted, with a flair for mathematics. In spite of his having to work much of the time, he graduated from Fort Smith High School in 1903 at the age of sixteen and promptly applied for admission to the University of Arkansas in Fayetteville, forty miles away. He was accepted.

During the next two years Savvy accomplished the spectacular feat of completing the University's four-year curriculum while at the same time supporting himself by working full-time on local road repair crews. For some reason the trustees of the University felt embarrassed by this achievement and passed a rule requiring four years of residency for graduation. Fortunately they decided not to apply the regulation to Savvy, perhaps because of a strong recommendation from his mathematics professor. Thus, in 1905 at age eighteen, Savvy Cooke graduated from college with a Bachelor of Science degree.

Eager to get as far away from Arkansas as possible, Savvy had already begun to plan his future. Through his reading he'd fallen under the influence of his maternal granduncle, Stephen Bleecker Luce, though he'd never met the old man. After rising to the highest level of command in the Navy at that time, Admiral Luce had retired from active duty to write a series of widely published essays espousing conservative political ideals and encouraging young men to enter the Navy. His writings found fertile ground in the mind of Charles Cooke Jr. and no doubt helped to shape the young man's character, as well as his career.

During his final months in college, Savvy applied for work with several large construction companies. He also wrote to one of Arkansas's state senators, asking for a recommendation to the U.S. Naval Academy at Annapolis. At this point, belatedly and indirectly, Savvy's father gave him a helping hand. Because of Charles Senior's long ago service to the state Democratic Party, the senator supported Savvy's application to the Naval Academy. The day after that letter arrived Savvy also received an attractive offer from a prominent Arkansas road-building company, but his mind was already made up. In June 1906 he began the two-day rail journey to Annapolis, Maryland.

Savvy liked the Navy from the beginning and he especially liked the Naval Academy. He didn't mind the school's rigid discipline or the grueling physical training, and he adapted easily to its demanding schedule, perhaps because it all seemed so much easier than growing up in Fort Smith. Intellectually he was in his element; the curriculum for midshipmen emphasized science, mathematics, and engineering, subjects for which he had a natural affinity. He reveled in the competition and constant testing, and achieved an excellent academic record. During his four years at the Academy only one other midshipman routinely surpassed him.

In spite of a pronounced Arkansas accent, Savvy also managed to overcome the widespread bias against Southerners that was prevalent at Annapolis and soon acquired a solid circle of friends. Although small in stature, he was quick and agile, and for two years played on the class baseball team. Each summer, along with the other midshipmen, he went on training cruises that shaped his

sea-going skills, introduced him to different types of ships, and fa-
miliarized him with seaports along the Atlantic coast. During the
second of these cruises Savvy met his old mentor, Admiral Luce,
who now lived in Portsmouth. The visit was the beginning of a
friendship that lasted until Luce died in 1917.

Savvy graduated from the Naval Academy in June 1910, finish-
ing second out of a class of 132. In those days graduates were not
automatically promoted to ensign, as they are today, but retained
the rank of midshipman (called "passed midshipman") until they
had served two years at sea. As a result Savvy didn't make ensign
until March 7, 1912, but after that his progress was rapid. Because
of his high class standing, he'd received a "plum" assignment right
out of the Academy as a gunnery officer on the U.S.S. *Connecticut,* the flagship of the Atlantic Fleet. The hours he spent in the
*Connecticut's* big gun turrets would ultimately cost Savvy some of
his hearing, but he would never regret them. Battleship duty was
valuable experience and a mark of distinction among naval officers.

As the second decade of the twentieth century began, Germany and Great Britain were engaged in a heated naval arms race.
Although the United States professed to be neutral, under Teddy
Roosevelt it had begun an aggressive program of naval expansion
that rivaled those of the European superpowers. A disciple of Alfred Thayer Mahan's 1890 classic *The Influence of Seapower in
History,* Roosevelt advocated a "big ship" navy while he was assistant secretary of the Navy in 1898. When he became president
after the assassination of William McKinley in 1901, he was able
to put this policy into high gear. By 1910 the Navy had commissioned sixteen large battleships with a commitment to build two
more of these floating fortresses every year.

For a young naval officer service in these great ships was the
surest road to advancement; and by 1913 Savvy Cooke had been
posted to three of the most prestigious battleships in the fleet, the
*Connecticut,* the *Maine,* and the *Alabama.* Having put in three
years of sea duty, he'd been promoted twice, with the likelihood of
further advancement in the near future. Savvy's prospects looked

bright, especially if he stuck with battleship duty, but he had different ideas.

While still a gunnery officer on the *Connecticut,* Savvy had applied for submarine school. To many of his contemporaries this must have seemed a poor choice. Submarine duty wasn't highly esteemed by the Navy's mainstream officer corps. Although the Navy had committed itself to building a submarine force, it hadn't spent much money on it. European nations had invested far more in their submarine programs and it showed in the number and quality of their boats. The French, Russian, and British navies each had roughly twice the number of subs as the U.S. Navy. On a technological level American subs weren't even in the same league as their European counterparts. And there was little evidence that this situation would change. In 1913 the Electric Boat Company, which built submarines for the Navy, was nearly bankrupt. By applying to sub school, Savvy Cooke was abandoning a promising career in the most spectacular ships afloat for a branch of the service that offered less glamour, less prestige, and significantly more danger. Nevertheless, he may have had good reasons for his decision.

Although it wasn't obvious at first, the rules of naval warfare were changing. For hundreds of years it had been a basic tenet of naval combat that the ship with the biggest guns and the heaviest armor usually won. The resulting race for size and power reached its zenith in the enormous battlewagons of the early twentieth century. These were—and still are—the largest floating gun platforms ever built; but even as they were launched, the era of the dreadnoughts was drawing to a close. Two inventions would spell its end: the submarine and (several decades later) the airplane.

The Germans were the first to realize the potential of submarine warfare, although they did so almost by accident. During the first year of the war, with the British navy firmly in control of the North Sea, the majority of German warships lay uselessly at anchor, bottled up in ports from Denmark to the Netherlands. In desperation the Germans turned to the submarine and soon discovered that their U-Boats could slip in and out of blockaded

ports almost at will. In addition these killer subs proved to be devastating against Allied shipping. During the first year of the war
they nearly brought England to her knees, sinking British mer-
chantmen almost faster than they could be built. The success of
the U-Boats was a great surprise to most naval authorities (including the Germans), but it shouldn't have been. The clues had been
there for years.

In September 1900, the Navy's very first sub, the U.S.S. *Holland*, while engaged in naval exercises off Newport, Rhode Island,
surprised the battleship *Kearsarge*, which was acting as flagship of
the "invading" fleet. Slipping in under cover of darkness, the little
submarine cheerfully signaled, "Hello, *Kearsarge*! You're blown
to atoms! This is the *Holland*." Less than a year later, the French
submarine *Gustav Zede* fired a dummy torpedo into the side of a
moving battleship to the "general stupefaction" of the battleship's
officers.

These and other demonstrations led British Admiral John
"Jacky" Fisher to write in 1904: "It is astounding to me, perfectly
astounding, how the very best amongst us fail to realize the vast
impending revolution in Naval warfare and Naval strategy that the
submarine will accomplish." Conservative naval officers on both
sides of the Atlantic ignored Admiral Fisher, but many younger
officers, like Chester Nimitz and Savvy Cooke, took his words to
heart. By going into submarines, they believed that they were riding the wave of the future.

On a more practical level Savvy may have been looking for an
early command. In the conventional Navy—the surface Navy—
even an officer of high rank and seniority could wait years for a
ship of his own; but, because of a shortage of qualified skippers,
the submarine service routinely gave command to junior officers.
For an ambitious young ensign like Savvy Cooke, subs would have
been a tempting shortcut. In fact, many of the officers in high
command during World War II started out as submarine captains
during World War I.

Money could have played a role in Savvy's decision too. Although officers didn't receive the "diving bonuses" that made the

service attractive for enlisted men, they did make a higher base salary. And at this point in his life Savvy needed a larger income. For some time he'd been courting a young woman named Helena Leslie Temple, the daughter of a prominent family from Philadelphia's Main Line. Savvy and Leslie (she went by her middle name) were married on April 30, 1913, in Brierly, Pennsylvania and honeymooned at Susina, a romantic old plantation near Thomasville, Georgia. Six months later, on November 17, 1913, Savvy reported to submarine school in New York Harbor aboard the battered old gunboat U.S.S. *Tonopah.*

The *Tonopah* was one of the last of the American monitors. Based on the famous ironclad that fought the Confederate *Merrimack* to a draw in 1862, these small battleships still featured the characteristic turret-mounted guns and flat decks lying flush with the water. Although the design had made sense in the days when naval guns fired heavy round shot, it had disastrous consequences for an ocean-going vessel. Offering no resistance to waves breaking onto their decks, their nonexistent freeboard caused monitors to roll and yaw horribly in heavy seas and kept their interiors wet and stifling.

In spite of their abysmal sea-keeping properties, monitors were still being used in combat by the British during World War I, but the U.S. Navy had long since converted its own monitors into sub-tenders and school ships. The *Tonopah* had seen better days. Before she became a floating classroom, she'd served as the flagship for Lieutenant Chester Nimitz, when he was commander of the Atlantic Submarine Flotilla.

For someone who had spent the past three years on the newest and biggest battleships in the fleet, the old ironclad and her brood of damp, malodorous little "pig boats" must have seemed like a significant step down, but Savvy accepted the change without complaint. For the next fourteen months he and his classmates pored over engineering blueprints and operations manuals, sat through countless lectures, and soon began to put their knowledge to work during practice cruises.

In those early days of the submarine program, a submarine

commander had to be a resourceful engineer, as well as a leader; equipment broke down frequently, parts and repairs were hard to come by, and skippers often had to display considerable ingenuity to keep their boats at sea. Once again Savvy was in his element, and he threw himself into his studies with his usual intelligence and enthusiasm. He could hardly have guessed it, but less than a year after his graduation from sub school, this hard-won knowledge would be severely tested . . . in a submarine called the *E-Two*.

### On board the *S-Five*, Wednesday, 15:25— Control Room.

Not long after the regulating pump was connected to the torpedo room, word came back that the water level in the bow was dropping. It was the first good news the crew had received since the *S-Five* went down, and a murmur of excited speculation swept through the boat.

Savvy didn't say anything to discourage the men, but he suspected that their high spirits were premature. After an hour and a half on the bottom, as far as he could tell, their chances for survival looked worse rather than better. Both of the sub's drive motors and both of her main pumps were now inoperative. Water was leaking rapidly into the sub through the main induction system and the only means they had of combating it was a low-capacity device that was only working because they were backing it up with their limited supply of compressed air. Even assuming that nothing else went wrong, Savvy doubted that the little regulating pump would ever float the sub; and even if it did, at the rate it was going, they'd exhaust their breathable air before that happened.

There was more bad news. Fred Whitehead had reported that two of the three air banks registered below 300 pounds pressure. The chief had just switched over to the last bank. Savvy was faced with an unpleasant dilemma: he could continue pressurizing the torpedo room so that the regulating pump would work, or he could save the compressed air as a breathing reserve and allow the flooding to continue. Whatever he decided, the time they had left was steadily ticking away.

Yet, it wasn't in Savvy's nature to give up. There had to be another way to get the submarine to the surface, something he hadn't tried yet. The only thing he could think of, however, was blowing the aft ballast tanks, and he'd put that off for a very good reason. Blowing the aft tanks would add buoyancy at the stern, while the excess weight from the flooding was still concentrated in the bow. The *S-Five* had already been through one near fatal experience because of unbalanced buoyancy due to the Kingstons. Savvy had no desire to risk another.

But he had no alternative.

The *S-Five* didn't have a public address system, but even if one had existed, Savvy probably wouldn't have used it to announce his decision. He didn't even warn the sailors who were standing near him in the control room that he was going to blow the aft tanks. Perhaps he didn't want to raise false hopes. Whatever his reasons may have been, the majority of the crew were unaware that Fred Whitehead had begun to feed compressed air into the tanks.

At first nothing happened. There were some faint sounds, but no apparent movement. When several seconds had passed without effect, Whitehead added more air, trying to break the grip of the sea floor.

He needn't have bothered. The stern had already lifted quietly off the bottom. The change was slight at first, too small for anyone on board to notice, but it had profound effects. For as the stern rose, the water in the bilges shifted slightly forward. This moved the sub's center of gravity a few inches toward the bow, which increased the rate of tilting, which sent still more water surging forward. And so on! By the time anyone realized that something was amiss, the chain reaction was completely out of control.

Savvy had been watching for trouble, but even he was unprepared for the explosiveness with which catastrophe struck. "Belay blowing!" he yelled. Fred Whitehead immediately began spinning control wheels to cut off the flow of compressed air, but the *S-Five* was already swinging ponderously up by the stern.

Faster and faster she rose. Unsecured objects began sliding and rolling toward the bow, smaller items bouncing into the air and raining down like shrapnel. Braced against the air manifold, Fred Whitehead was in no danger of falling, but he found himself pelted by flying debris and several times had to move quickly to avoid heavier projectiles that smashed into the bulkhead. The sub was filled with a growing cacophony, a combination of the rattling and crashing from within and the grating rumble of the bow pivoting on the bottom.

## 15:30—Motor Room.

Standing in the motor room doorway, Chief Bender looked down the long central aisle between the diesels and could only imagine that the sub had slipped off the edge of an underwater cliff and was sliding into deeper water. He was staring at the hull in morbid fascination, waiting for the inevitable implosion and wondering if he would even see it coming, when one of the engineers tugged at his sleeve and pointed aft. Turning, Bender looked into the motor room, where a pair of replacement heads for the diesels had been lashed onto an overhead rack.

"I can just see those coming down through the boat, Chief!" the sailor said.

Bender could picture it too. With the sub tilted this steeply, those cylinder heads would turn into deadly missiles. The immediate threat took his mind off the fate of the hull and he joined the engineer behind the motor room bulkhead.

## 15:30—Control Room.

When the angle of the deck passed thirty degrees, it became impossible to stand. Crewmen who couldn't find something to hang on to began sliding toward the bow. At the switchboard in the control room, Otto grabbed the periscope guides and hung on. And then, just when it seemed things were at their worst, the tons of water and oil hidden in the bilges erupted from beneath the floor and the interior of the sub dissolved into a nightmare.

Spilling onto the forward bulkheads and swirling through the narrow doorways, the water roared down the sloping decks in a growing flood that picked up everything that wasn't tied down and carried it forward: boxes, books, tools, deck plates, floor mats, and men, all went tumbling toward the bow, accompanied by a monstrous rattling and shaking of the entire sub.

In the forward end of the control room a small group of sailors tried valiantly to close the battery room door, but the flood's leading edge overwhelmed them, scattered them into the corners and pinned the watertight door back against the forward bulkhead.

The water knocked Ramon Otto off his feet, wrenched his hands away from the periscope guides, and swept him down against the bulkhead. In an instant he was sucked through the doorway into the battery room. Arms and legs flailing, he tried to find the surface, but he was enveloped in a blinding maelstrom of water, oil, and foam that obscured any sense of direction. Unable to see, unable to breathe, battered and bruised as the currents slammed him into things, he thought fleetingly that a manhole cover on one of the ballast tanks must have been carried away. The sub was foundering and he was going to die. The realization brought regret and sorrow more than fear. *What will Maud do?* He was running out of air now, chest burning, throat knotted, diaphragm beginning to twitch uncontrollably; at any moment he'd inhale in spite of himself.

*Very well,* he thought, *let's get it over with!*—and he opened his mouth . . .

SAVVY AND FRED WHITEHEAD clung to the air manifold. With the reduced lighting and the water and debris that filled the air, it was impossible to see anything clearly. One after another crewmen tumbled down the deck to land in the water that had backed up against the forward bulkhead. Some disappeared into the whirlpool over the battery room door. Others found handholds and pulled themselves to safety. John Longstaff landed nearby with a tremendous splash, surfaced sputtering and swearing, and battled his way to the conning tower ladder, where he managed to climb out of the flood's reach.

At one point the water rose past Savvy's neck. Hauling himself higher on the air manifold, he wondered briefly how long this would continue. If it didn't stop soon, water would fill the battery room and begin flooding the control room too. Losing this compartment, the sub's nerve center, would be the ultimate disaster. They'd be cut off from the main switchboard, the air manifold, the regulating pump . . .

In the middle of the compartment Charlie Grisham hung on near his station at the speaking tubes. He was out of harm's way here, but he decided to do something about the flooding. Swinging out into the center of the compartment he tried to force his way up to the engine room door, but the waist-high water, moving with the speed of a mill race, forced him back to the speaking tubes.

As he prepared for a second attempt, someone passed him. It was electrician Walter Nelson, swimming uphill through the solid flow of water. At any moment it appeared the cascade would fling him back into the welter of water and trash on the forward bulkhead, but somehow the young electrician managed to keep moving. Scrabbling with his feet and thrashing his arms, he fought his way up to the aft bulkhead, but there he was stopped. No matter how hard he strained, he couldn't pull himself through the doorway. Exhausted, his grip failing, he was about to slide back when a long arm reached down from the engine room, grabbed his shirt, and yanked him through.

### 15:31—Battery Room.

As Otto began to take a breath, his head broke the surface and he inhaled air instead of water. The *S-Five* hadn't flooded after all.

Instead, he'd fallen into a pool that was forming in the forward end of the battery room, already so deep that he couldn't touch bottom. Gasping and choking, his eyes and throat burning from the reek of diesel oil, Otto struggled blindly until his hand struck a metal stanchion and he was able to drag himself partly out of the water.

After that he simply hung on, working his way higher as the water level rose, and wondered when, or if, the flooding would stop. Far above he could see the open doorway leading into the control room and possible safety, but he had no strength to get there. One of the sailors near him tried to scramble up the deck and might have made it, if a box of supplies hadn't broken loose and knocked him head over heels back into the water. He crawled up beside Otto with a glazed look in his eyes. Another sailor had taken refuge on one of the top bunks, just under the forward main ballast vent. The air was stifling, and it was more than just diesel fumes; Otto could see a kind of heavy fog rising above the water. Then he knew what it was. The battery wells had been breached. The mist was deadly chlorine gas!

### 15:31—Engine Room.

As he sagged against the coaming of the engine room doorway, Nelson saw that he'd been rescued by Machinist's Mate John Smith, who was at that moment trying to close the watertight door. As soon as Nels had caught his breath, he pitched in to help, but for some reason the door wouldn't shut. They wasted several seconds in futile wrestling before running their hands around the door rim. One of the dogging levers had jammed.

Nelson scrabbled around in the water-soaked rubbish that covered the bulkhead, found a metal bar, and handed it to Smith, who battered the dog loose. Looking down into the engine room, they saw Lieutenant Grisham, who had trailed Nelson up through the control room; but, when he saw them holding the door for him, the he called out, "Close it!" An instant later the door pivoted into place with a resounding thump.

## 15:32—Control Room.

When the door to the engine room slammed shut, the rush of water stopped, as if it had been cut off by a tap. John Longstaff slid down from his perch on the conning tower ladder, jumped onto the forward bulkhead and tipped its watertight door up and over, sealing off the battery room from further flooding. The remaining water began to form an oily pool in the angle between the deck and the forward bulkhead. Gingerly the crew began to pick themselves up from wherever they had landed and, for the second time in as many hours, looked around wonderingly at what had become of their world.

Except for puddles everywhere, the sinking two hours earlier hadn't changed the sub's appearance much, but now the *S-Five* had undergone an astonishing transformation. She was literally standing on end, with her bow jammed into the seafloor and her hull angled upward as steeply as a household stepladder. Forward bulkheads had become weirdly canted floors, while aft bulkheads were tilted ceilings forty feet overhead.

Rubble was everywhere, scattered in piles or stuffed into corners and crevices, wherever the receding water had left it. Jammed against the air manifold, Savvy Cooke and Fred Whitehead struggled to free themselves from the mass of boxes and cocoa-fiber deck mats that had nearly buried them. Savvy was anxious to find out about his crew, especially the men in the battery compartment. In addition to the handful who'd been there before the aft tanks were blown, he'd seen several more get sucked through the doorway during the flooding. As soon as he'd extricated himself from the clinging mats, he scrambled across to the watertight door and peered down through the porthole. The glass was smeared with oil and the light was poor, but he saw enough to confirm his fears.

"Help me open this door!"

Longstaff and Whitehead jumped to help. It required all three of them to lift the door, which by now was covered with several inches of water; but by hoisting together they pulled it up and over.

Twenty feet below them nearly a dozen men clung to the sides of the compartment or struggled to stay afloat in the pool that had formed at its forward end. The air was heavy with the smell of bleach, the characteristic odor of chlorine gas.

"Come on!" Savvy said. "Let's get those men out now!"

# 6

## VERTICAL WORLD

"In comradeship is danger countered best."
—JOHANN WOLFGANG VON GOETHE

WEDNESDAY, 15:40—BATTERY ROOM.

For the dozen or so sailors trapped in it, the battery room had become a hellish place. The pool that half-filled the compartment was choked with trash and covered by a layer of diesel fuel and oil, a noxious mixture that penetrated eyes, ears, nose, and mouth, and coated objects with a slippery residue that made it next to impossible to hold on to anything. Blinded and gagging, the stranded sailors had to struggle just to stay afloat. Some of them had been able to pull themselves partway out of the water onto bunks or piping, and a few of these men were trying to fit gas masks onto their faces; but most of them had no protection. And every minute the stench of chlorine gas was growing stronger.

At first it seemed impossible that anyone could escape. The steeply slanted walls were covered with oil, especially in the narrow passageway below the door, yet after it was opened, two of the more acrobatic sailors lunged from an upper bunk, grabbed the tie-down straps on the mess tables at the end of the compartment, and swung themselves high enough to be caught and hauled to safety. Others who tried to scramble after them merely slid back helplessly into the tangle of bodies thrashing about below. The longer this went on the more desperate and exhausted the trapped men became. For once Savvy was at a loss what to do. And then . . .

"I have an idea!" John Longstaff said. He clambered quickly up past the periscopes and tore down the curtains used to create the "officers' wardroom." When he brought them back down to the doorway and knotted them together, they made an effective "rope." Within a short time all of the stranded men had been pulled to safety, including poor Henry Love, who had been half-drowned for the second time that day.

Before the watertight door could be closed, someone had to climb down to make sure that everyone had been evacuated and to close the speaking tubes and battery vents in the compartment. Even though he couldn't find a gas mask to fit, Longstaff volunteered. Tying his makeshift rope to the door handle, he took a deep breath and swung down. It actually took him less than a minute to accomplish what he had to do, but by the time he climbed back up, his nose and throat were on fire. The chlorine was stronger than he'd expected.

### 16:00—Control Room.

Several of the rescued men were in bad shape. One young sailor from rural Pennsylvania had already begun to show signs of lung injury, coughing and wheezing and complaining that he couldn't get enough air; and the Filipino mess attendant had been struck by a door, probably fracturing some of his ribs. Henry Love was shaking again and appeared confused. One of his buddies helped him climb up to the conning tower, where he might be able to lie down.

Savvy regretted the injuries, but he was grateful that none of them were life-threatening. This was remarkable, considering the fact that many of the crew had fallen the length of more than one compartment, bouncing off machinery and narrowly missing any number of sharp edges and pointed objects.

After caring for their injured shipmates, the crew spread out through the control room, trying to find places to rest, but it was as if some two dozen men had taken up residence in a partly flooded elevator shaft. There was hardly a level surface to be found. The forward bulkhead was the nearest thing to a deck, but it was small and, in addition, crowded with pipes and valves and half-covered by a pool of filthy water.

In the end the sailors achieved security, if not comfort, by setting their backs against the nearly vertical deck and bracing their feet on the nearest piece of equipment. A lucky few managed to drape themselves along horizontal sections of piping or ductwork, or perched on the chart table. Everyone looked wet and cold, and many of them sported bumps and bruises. With their smudged faces and oily, tattered clothing, they presented a sorry sight. Longstaff couldn't restrain a chuckle at their expense and many found themselves smiling along with him in spite of their misery. Even Savvy Cooke flashed one of his rare grins, prompting a sailor to remark, "Mr. Longstaff, the captain's laughing, so I guess we will get out some way."

There were twenty-eight people in the control room, leaving twelve men, a third of the crew, cut off from them in the engine room. Luckily these included two of the S-*Five*'s most capable CPOs, Bill Bender and Reb Hutson, so Savvy could rely on competent leadership in that end of the boat. Nevertheless, looking up at the engine room bulkhead thirty-five feet overhead, he decided that the next order of business was to open that watertight door and reunite his crew.

Like everything else since the crash dive, this goal proved to be elusive. Merely climbing up to the door was a challenge. Everything was slick with oil and there were few hand- or footholds. Savvy had to weave from side to side, searching for support like a rock climber ascending a cliff. When he reached the bulkhead, he leaned out and pushed up on the door, but it wouldn't move. At first he thought it might be locked, but a quick inspection of the dogging levers showed that it wasn't. By this time Percy Fox had climbed up to help. Hanging out precariously over the long drop to the forward bulkhead, the Chief put his big shoulder under the door and thrust upward, but even his added strength was insufficient. In fact, no matter how many men swarmed up under the bulkhead to heave at the door, it wouldn't budge.

Eventually Savvy called off the attempt. As he watched Fox and the others climb back down to the forward end of the compartment, he brooded about the failure. Designed to withstand more than sixty pounds per square inch of pressure, the sub's watertight doors were heavy, but they weren't *that* heavy. Something else must be holding the door shut, perhaps a pile of rubble.

Savvy lowered himself carefully down to the forward bulkhead, mindful of the fact that merely moving around in this once-familiar space could be dangerous. It was a forty-foot fall from the aft end of the compartment. Many of the crew were perched nearly that high and some of their roosts looked rather precarious. He checked his watch and shook his head in frustration. It was 5:00 P.M., three hours since the crash dive and they were no closer to safety. As he'd feared, blowing the aft ballast tanks had been a fiasco, and as a result, he was now cut off from the aft end of the boat.

Just then Charlie Grisham scrambled down to sit beside him. While Savvy and Fox had struggled with the engine room door, Charlie had climbed up to the voice tubes to contact Bender and Hutson in the engine room. It had been a strenuous conversation for Charlie, because each time he wanted to speak or to listen, he had to pull himself up to the voice tube with both hands, as if he were doing a chin-up, but he'd stuck with it.

According to Chief Bender, Charlie said, the men in the stern section were uninjured and morale was good. In addition, the watertight door was being held shut by a pool of water four or five feet deep. Savvy kicked himself mentally; he should have considered that possibility, but at least it made the solution straightforward. They'd connect the regulating pump to the engine room bilges and soon the door could be opened.

Before Savvy could issue the order, however, with the appalling timing he'd almost come to expect, the regulating pump emitted a shrill whine. Savvy and Grisham exchanged worried looks. Except for a small hand pump in one of the equipment lockers, the regulating pump was their last way to get water out of the sub. Without it they'd be trapped as helplessly as the Japanese sailors in *Boat #6*.

Grisham wasted no time in disassembling the pump. To his immense relief, there was nothing wrong with it. The problem was in the torpedo room. When the *S-Five* pitched up on her nose, the water in the forward compartment shifted toward the bow; and as the regulating pump lowered the water level further, it uncovered the aft bilge drain, the one that Henry Love had opened before he left the compartment. As air was sucked into the system, the pump began to cavitate, and pumping action stopped.

It was simple and it was ironic. Love had made the correct decision in opening that drain; but the system had been intended for a *horizontal* submarine. How could Love—or the engineers who'd designed the *S-Five*—have foreseen that the sub would wind up standing on end?

Ironic or not, the regulating pump had done all it could in the torpedo room. Savvy told Grisham to switch it to the engine room. To avoid the problem they'd just encountered, he sent word to Hutson and Bender to close all the aft bilge drains and open the forward ones. This wouldn't be an easy assignment. The water in the bilges was deep and thick with sludge and assorted garbage. At first the engineering gang thought they'd have to dive headfirst into the repulsive mess to reach the valves for the forward drains. Then John Smith discovered that he could reach the valves with his toes without putting his face under water. This was an unusual role reversal for the lanky Smith, who was more often at a disadvantage because of his size.

By 5:30 they had gotten the pump switched over to the engine room. At first it worked well, but after a few minutes it began to strain and overheat. When Charlie and the engineers took it apart, they found that the wire inlet filter was clogged with crud from the water. They cleaned the filter, reassembled the pump and turned it on, whereupon it promptly clogged again . . . and yet again. As they reassembled the pump for the third time, one of the machinists suggested leaving the filter out.

This was a hard call. If they ran the pump without a filter, it might jam on a piece of trash and wreck its impellor. Charlie turned to the Captain and asked what they should do.

"Take it out!" he said.

So they discarded the filter, and the pump ran well. It didn't jam again, and within an hour it had lowered the water level in the engine room bilges by nearly three feet. Another foot or two and they'd be able to open the door into the engine room.

Savvy leaned against the soggy heap of deck mats beside the air manifold and tried to decide what to do next. In spite of missteps, they'd made progress of a sort. The control room's depth gauge now read sixty-two feet. By inadvertently tilting the S-five up on her nose, they had lifted the conning tower more than two thirds of the way to the surface. At first glance this seemed like a huge step, but Savvy knew better than to overestimate it. The water pressure on the conning tower hatch was still more than ten tons. They'd never be able to force it open and, even if they could, the sea would start pouring in immediately. They'd be lucky to get two or three men out before the sub took everyone else to the bottom. A better chance would be to try the motor room hatch, which was forty feet closer to the stern than the conning tower; but even that was more than thirty feet below the surface.

It was 6:00 P.M. Sunset was at 6:30 at this time of year. They obviously wouldn't get back to the surface in time to see it! Savvy thought about all that had happened since the crash dive. In some ways it was hard to believe they'd been underwater for only four hours. The thought prompted another question: how much time did they have left?

Normally the crew of an S-class submarine could go several days without surfacing, but a lot had happened to reduce that potential for the *S-Five*. Their largest air reserve was the interior of the sub itself, but they'd already been forced to abandon two compartments. Taking into account the flooding in the rest of the sub, the internal volume had probably been cut in half.

Then there were the air banks. Ordinarily these could be counted as reserves, too, but according to Chief Whitehead only one of the *S-Five*'s air banks was still pressurized, and they'd need that one to fight the leak in the torpedo room.

The *S-Five* had also been equipped with the new air purification canisters that had been developed during the war. These contained carbon dioxide absorbing salts and reserve oxygen cylinders, but the main canister in the *S-Five* had been installed in the torpedo room! The remaining cannisters, over the chart table in the control room and another in the engine room, were quite small.

Savvy shook his head ruefully. If he ever got out of this, he'd have a number of suggestions for the *S-Five*'s designers, such as putting air canisters in *every* compartment, but there was nothing to be done about it now. Putting all of their resources together, he estimated that the *S-Five* had enough breathable air for another day and a half or perhaps two days at the most. Then what?

Savvy knew the answer to that question only too well. When the oxygen level inside the sub fell to less than half its normal value, men would begin to die. But there was more to it than that, because lack of oxygen doesn't hurt. It just makes people feel drowsy. If a room were filled with normal air from which all the oxygen had been removed, you could walk inside and fall down dead without feeling the least discomfort.

Carbon dioxide was different. Even low levels of the gas made people feel lousy. Normal air contained very little carbon dioxide, but humans exhaled it nearly as fast as they used up oxygen, so it built up rapidly when people were in closed spaces. Even now the level inside the *S-Five* was probably two or three times higher than normal. At any moment Savvy expected to feel short of breath. That was the first symptom.

It got worse.

By the time the carbon dioxide level in the sub had risen to ten times normal, Savvy and his men would be panting like sprinters, just to keep the stuff from building up in their bloodstreams. As the level rose still higher, they wouldn't be able to breathe fast enough. Then carbon dioxide would begin to accumulate inside them, making their blood acidic, disrupting their internal chemistry, making nearly every organ in their bodies malfunction.

This last stage was marked by increasing misery: blurred vision, dizziness, headaches, heart palpitations, tremors and muscle spasms—but worst of all, by an aching and unquenchable hunger for air that eventually made unconsciousness a blessing. In the end the *S-Five*'s crew would die from lack of oxygen, but carbon dioxide would torture them horribly before that happened.

It was hard to avoid morbid thinking. Right now their only effective resource, the regulating pump, was still making headway in the engine room, but Savvy knew that wouldn't suffice. The torpedo room contained more than enough water to keep the sub on the bottom and the regulating pump no longer worked there. They simply had to find some other way to get that water out. For the hundredth time Savvy wracked his brain, searching for a new approach, something he'd missed.

Finally an idea occurred to him. Instead of trying to *pull* the water out of the torpedo room through the drainage system, why not *push* it out the way it had come in? The more he considered the possibility, the better he liked it. Beckoning Charlie Grisham to follow, he climbed over to the air manifold, where Fred Whitehead had propped himself. "How much air do we have, Chief?"

According to Whitehead the last air bank still contained nearly 500 p.s.i. If they were careful it might be enough to achieve what Savvy had in mind. A few minutes later the chief began feeding additional compressed air into the torpedo room, while Grisham recruited Percy Fox to climb up to the main induction valve with

him. They were going to open it, a task that Charlie found especially distasteful, considering how hard they'd worked to close it in
the first place. But, when he put his ear to the valve a few minutes
later, he heard water beginning to flow, as the increased air pressure in the torpedo room forced it into the ventilator duct and all
the way back through the main induction system into the sea.
Charlie had to admire Savvy's scheme. By reversing the flow of
water in the main induction system, it stopped the leak at the
same time that it expelled water from the sub.

By this time Savvy had moved on to another project. Using the
voice tubes to tell Smith and the other sailors in the engine room
which valves to open and close, he and Fred Whitehead were
pressurizing the fuel tanks one by one and using transfer lines to
shunt the last of the sub's diesel fuel out into the sea. Besides light-
ening the sub further, the oil would form a wide slick on the surface, which might attract the attention of a passing ship.

IT WAS TEN MINUTES BEFORE 7:00. The S-*Five* had been on
the bottom for five hours. Savvy ran through a mental inventory:
torpedo room, engine room, fuel tanks . . . all pieces in a puzzle, a
deadly serious puzzle, where the stakes were life or death.

Sitting beside the depth gauge in the middle of the control
room, John Longstaff had begun tapping it with a screwdriver to
keep the needle from sticking and "singing out" the new readings
every quarter of a foot. Sixty-one feet . . . sixty . . . fifty-nine. . . .
At this rate, the sub might lift off the bottom at any moment. Once
that happened, it would only be a matter of time until the motor
room hatch broke the surface. Then they'd climb out into the
fresh air, deploy the life rafts, and start thinking about attracting a
ship. They wouldn't be saved by any means, but at least they'd be
out under the open sky, and at this point almost anything seemed
preferable to remaining inside this great steel casket waiting for
their air to run out.

Beneath his iron self-control, Savvy must have felt a cautious
sense of optimism. In spite of all the bad breaks, in spite of the po-

tential at every turn for a fatal mistake that would have killed everyone in his command, he'd persevered. Soon, if all went well, they'd take another huge step toward survival. For Savvy, saving his crew had to be a deeply personal goal, because there had been a time, not long before this, when all his knowledge and all his care had *not* been enough.

# 7

## THE *E-TWO*

"Let us not burden our remembrance with a heaviness
that's gone."
                                          —WILLIAM SHAKESPEARE

AS CHIEF ELECTRICIAN on the *S-Five*, Ramon Otto was accustomed to staying busy. Submarines depended on electricity to
an extraordinary degree. Electricity drove the propellers during
dives, ran the pumps and the air compressors, spun the ventilation
fans and the flywheels in the gyroscopes, and moved the
periscopes up and down. It powered the interior lights and
heaters, lit the navigation beacons, and energized the radio and
the galley appliances. Electricity even helped to launch the torpedoes.

Linking all these devices was a maze of wiring, miles of it, together with gauges, switches, circuit breakers and fuses, huge batteries to supply the current, and motors that could act as
generators to recharge those batteries. To top it off, the entire
complex system had to function in an environment so hostile to
electrical equipment that it was sometimes a wonder anything
worked. Continually exposed to salt, moisture, and extremes of
temperature, the electrical systems on a submarine required constant maintenance. To provide that level of support every crew in-

cluded a full complement of electricians headed by a chief petty officer like Ramon.

Of all the devices Otto and his men had to manage, probably none was more demanding than the electrical storage batteries. Lead-acid cells, the type used in submarines, had changed little since their invention half a century earlier. A single lead-acid cell consisted of alternating plates of lead and lead oxide in a dilute solution of sulfuric acid.[7] The *S-Five* was equipped with 120 of these cells, each weighing half a ton, arranged in groups of sixty in a well three feet deep beneath the battery room floor.

Durable and inexpensive, lead-acid batteries could supply large amounts of current over long periods of time, an important characteristic in vessels that needed to travel long distances underwater; but, as Ray Otto knew all too well, they also had disadvantages. For one thing, the lead plates made them extremely heavy. For another, as they generated electricity, a simultaneous chemical reaction called hydrolysis split the water inside them into its constituent hydrogen and oxygen. The oxygen didn't pose much of a problem, but hydrogen is an exceedingly flammable gas. (In 1937 it would be responsible for the explosion of the airship *Hindenburg* over Lakehurst, New Jersey.) To keep hydrogen gas from building up to explosive levels inside submarines, the battery wells had to be thoroughly ventilated. At the same time, however, they had to be protected from seawater, because the salt in seawater would react with the sulfuric acid in the batteries to produce poisonous chlorine gas.

As a final complication, the water lost due to hydrolysis had to be replaced at regular intervals. This process—called "watering" the batteries—was tedious and unpleasant because of the fumes from the acid. It could be dangerous, as well. In spite of their low voltage, the cells could deliver a fatal shock.

The competing requirements for battery design made a formidable engineering problem that was never perfectly solved. When Ray Otto joined the submarine service in 1913, battery room

---

[7] Most automotive batteries today are of the lead-acid type.

decks were made of removable wooden shutters covered by a layer of rubberized canvas. Several years later the Bureau of Construction and Repair substituted steel deck plates with rubber gaskets. These plates were safer, but harder to remove for maintenance. Engineering officers complained so bitterly about the change that the old-fashioned wooden decking was reinstated.

In the majority of subs the battery wells were ventilated by electric fans that drew air in on one side of the compartment and expelled it on the other.[8] Through some engineering shortsightedness, in the early S-Boats the ventilation ports weren't equipped with isolation valves. Instead they were sealed by cover plates that had to be bolted on by hand, a time-consuming process that offered little protection in an emergency. In many subs the electricians didn't even bother to keep the cover plates beside the ports. When Savvy Cooke took command of the *S-Five*, he issued an order that cover plates were to be hung on the mounting bolts beside each port. Some of the electricians grumbled about the extra attention this required, but Ramon understood. The captain—and Ramon too—had every reason to be sensitive about battery safety considering what had happened during Savvy's first command.

WHEN SAVVY FINISHED submarine school in the Spring 1915, he embarked on a busy year. He'd already learned in December that he'd been picked for early promotion to the rank of lieutenant junior grade, and that his first submarine assignment would be as executive officer on a brand new sub called the *K-Two*. But he didn't know how soon he'd move on from there. Within a month he received orders to another submarine, called the *E-Two*. But this time he'd report aboard as the sub's commanding officer.

From junior officer to command in only a few months was an impressive achievement, but Savvy had more than his ability to thank. His rapid rise to captain was partly the result of the high

[8] In the *S-Five* the inlets were on the starboard side and the outlets on the port side.

turnover among submarine officers. The *E-Two* was a prime example. In December, during naval exercises off Rhode Island, the four-year-old *E-Two* (originally the *Sturgeon*) was running submerged at a depth of fifty feet, when seawater infiltrated her battery well. A cloud of chlorine gas swept through the sub, nearly overpowering her crew. They managed to surface and open the conning tower hatch in time to save themselves, but they were so incapacitated that the *E-Two* had to be towed into port. Her skipper's lungs were so badly damaged that he would require nearly a year to recover. Savvy was chosen as his replacement.

Savvy's first few months as captain were uneventful, or almost so. In the spring, along with the rest of the Atlantic Fleet, the *E-Two* paid a visit to New York Harbor. The third day of their visit was cool and cloudless, the kind of weather that brought crowds of sightseers to the downtown waterfront on the Hudson where the Navy ships had moored. Savvy was standing with several other officers on the deck of the *Tonopah,* his former school ship, when the wake of a passing tour boat swamped a nearby canoe and swept its occupants, two teenage boys, in among the pilings of the pier.

One of the boys appeared to be trapped under the overturned boat. Without hesitation Savvy leaped into the frigid water. Holding on to the pier with one hand, he pulled the trapped youth from beneath the canoe, then supported both boys until sailors from a nearby submarine threw a rope and a boat was brought around from the *Tonopah.* The rescue made local headlines, but the remainder of the summer passed without incident and Savvy began to settle comfortably into his new role as skipper.

Meanwhile his marriage was not going well. Leslie had come from a "society" family, part of Philadelphia's upper crust. It isn't clear what she'd expected from marriage to an ambitious and dedicated Navy officer, but it certainly wasn't what she found. Savvy's long absences and frequent preoccupation with military matters quickly become a source of conflict. He did what he could to minimize Leslie's disappointments, but all too often the needs of the

Navy had to come first. And so, in spite of their affection for each other, they began to drift apart. Then in July Leslie told him that she was pregnant. Under the circumstances, the news that they were about to become parents was a mixed blessing.

As if that weren't complication enough, in August Savvy was informed that the *E-Two* had been chosen to test the new Edison Submarine Battery.

THE FIRST BATTERY-POWERED AUTOMOBILE was built in 1834. By the end of the century the United States supported a thriving market for electrically powered cars. Initially the only source of electricity for them was the same type of lead-acid battery that was used in submarines, even though they were less suitable in cars. They were too heavy and their voltage faded as they discharged.[9]

America's premier inventor at the turn of the century, Thomas Alva Edison, decided to address this problem. In 1900 he began working on an alternative type of automobile battery. Edison had already produced an impressive list of innovations including the phonograph, the stock ticker, the motion picture camera, and the first practical incandescent light bulb. By 1909 he had added the world's first alkaline battery to the list.

In place of lead and lead oxide, the new Edison Battery employed iron and nickel oxide; instead of a sulfuric acid electrolyte, it contained caustic potash (potassium hydroxide); and instead of a soft lead lining it was encased in steel. The new battery was more efficient, more stable and longer lasting than its lead-acid competitor. In spite of costing about three times as much as an equivalent lead-acid battery, it was an immediate success. But for once Edison's timing was off. The internal-combustion engine was al-

[9] The reader should note that modern internal combustion engine cars employ lead-acid batteries for short-term bursts of current to run their starter motors or to provide auxiliary power when the engine isn't running. They don't use their batteries for propulsion, as true electric cars do.

ready well on its way to dominating the automobile power industry. At a time when cars like the ubiquitous Model T were started with a hand crank, this left no role for the Edison battery. The inventor began looking for another market.

In June, 1910, Edison's assistant and principal business partner, Miller Reese Hutchison, visited the Naval Academy to consult on a new form of tachometer (to measure engine speed) in submarines. Although not as brilliant as Edison, Hutchison had a number of inventions to his credit, including the Klaxon horn that was used on Navy ships to sound alarms. He was also a keen businessman and an aggressive promoter of Edison's interests. During his visit Hutchison went along on several demonstration dives, during which he learned of the shortcomings of lead-acid batteries. According to an account given in a promotional brochure published by the Edison Battery Company in 1915, shortly after Hutchison's Annapolis visit, several Navy officers asked Edison to adapt his new battery for use in submarines. By 1915 the necessary modification and laboratory testing had been done, and the battery was ready for field testing.

Prior to 1915 Edison had contributed occasional inventions to the military, including a wire-guided torpedo, but in general he had confined himself to peacetime applications. After the sinking of the passenger ship *Lusitania* by a German U-Boat on May 7 of that year, the inventor gave a long interview to the *New York Times* in which he recommended establishment of a civilian research laboratory to guarantee military superiority over the Germans. At that time the secretary of the navy was Josephus Daniels, a former newspaper editor from North Carolina and a Christian pacifist, who knew little about military matters. (Daniels had qualified himself for the post primarily by supporting Woodrow Wilson's 1912 presidential campaign.) His relationship with the military was never cordial and he often relied on subordinates, particularly his energetic and aristocratic assistant secretary, Franklin D. Roosevelt, to deal with the Navy's brass.

After reading Edison's 1915 interview in the *Times*, Daniels realized that the inventor shared his dim view of military brass, whom Edison characterized as having "no imagination." Daniels invited Edison to head the newly formed Naval Consulting Board, a panel of civilians and military officers that would guide naval development. Not long afterwards the Edison Battery was scheduled for testing in Navy submarines. The boat chosen to perform the tests was the *E-Two*.

In many ways the Edison Battery was ideal for submarines. It was more stable and more reliable than its lead-acid cousin; its nickel-plated steel construction resisted the kind of battery leaks that had sunk the *Skate* in March of that very year; and substitution of caustic potash for sulfuric acid eliminated the danger of chlorine gas that had nearly doomed the *E-Two* herself. Other than its expense, the battery had only one major drawback.

Like the lead-acid battery, the Edison battery generated hydrogen gas, but there was an important difference. Lead-acid cells gave off hydrogen when they were *discharging,* while Edison's battery did so when it was *charging.* Unconcerned by this difference, Edison and his engineers claimed that the same venting procedures effective for lead-acid cells would control the hydrogen produced by their battery. It seemed like a reasonable assumption at the time.

IN AUGUST 1915, Miller Hutchison arrived at the Brooklyn Navy Yard, bringing with him several assistants and a large amount of equipment. Hutchison wasted no time in setting up shop at the Brooklyn wharf. Secretary Daniels's office had paved the way for him by instructing the officers of the Navy Yard to cooperate with Edison's staff in every way.

On August 30, the Second Submarine Flotilla sailed into New York Harbor, and Savvy pulled the *E-Two* up to Brooklyn's old Number Two Dock, where the testing would take place. During the next few weeks workmen from the yard assisted the submarine's crew in removing her original lead-acid batteries and installing 240 Edison cells, half of them in a forward compartment and half of them in the stern.

Testing began near the end of September, at first while the sub was moored to the dock and later at sea. It was tedious work. As the batteries were charged and discharged the electricians had to keep detailed records of voltage and current, to be compared with experimental data from Edison's New Jersey laboratory. Savvy worked hard to achieve optimal performance from the battery. In a letter to Edison during the first weeks of testing, Hutchison described the *E-Two*'s captain as "a very earnest, industrious young man," and added, "I am very much impressed with him." But from the outset the young lieutenant had misgivings about the new batteries. He was concerned about the hydrogen gas given off during charging and he suspected that Hutchison's ventilating and cooling system was inadequate.

For the next four months Savvy tried every means at his disposal to improve the safety of the installation. He wrote letters through the chain of command, cautioning against the dangers of hydrogen gas. His warnings were ignored. He requested measuring devices to track the hydrogen content of the cells. The request was denied. He tried to install individual voltage meters for each cell, to show which ones might generate gas. Hutchison vetoed the change, insisting that individual meters would increase the likelihood of damaging short circuits. Savvy even went so far as to circumvent the chain of command, a risky step in the military, by asking navy chemists to install hydrogen gas detectors in the battery wells; but the chemists couldn't find or build instruments that were sensitive enough to do the job. There seemed to be nothing that Savvy could do.

Sea trials began on Long Island Sound in November. During the following weeks, several minor explosions occurred in the battery compartments. To Savvy's consternation, Hutchison dismissed the detonations as insignificant, but he did agree to conduct accurate measurements of the hydrogen gas. Savvy must have expected the test to support his viewpoint; but the chief chemist from the Navy's Bureau of Steam Engineering reported only "infinitesimal" amounts of hydrogen in the battery wells. He concluded that this indicated a safe level.

Savvy felt that *any* detectable hydrogen was a bad sign, but the chemist's report certainly didn't help his case. In desperation the *E-Two*'s captain intercepted some of the drawings for the ventilation system and added his own changes to increase their capacity. When Hutchison learned of this, he complained directly to Secretary Daniels's office. As a result Savvy's changes were discarded and the engineers at the yard were forbidden to follow his suggestions.

Near the end of December several of the power profiles for the batteries showed insufficient capacity. Hutchison decided to remedy this by forcing the cells through a complete charge and discharge cycle, which would thicken the current generating chemical layers on the metal plates. To do this he would link the two groups of cells together, connect them to the yard's power supply and drive them through the sequence in a single day.

Within two weeks the yard's workmen had prepared the experiment, which would take place over the weekend of January 16, 1916. On Friday, the 15th, Savvy gave the majority of the *E-Two*'s crew weekend liberty, so that only a skeleton staff of electricians and yard workmen would remain on board. On Saturday the discharge phase began at 10:00 A.M. During this cycle, the sub's electricians would monitor battery performance and "water" the cells, adding enough fresh water to bring the potassium hydroxide solution up to the proper level.

The tragedy that began to brew in the *E-Two*'s dimly lighted interior that morning originated in a subtle aspect of battery operation. With all the cells linked together, it was possible for some of them to discharge completely and then to begin charging again using current from the remainder of the cells which were still in the discharge phase. During initial laboratory trials, Edison's technicians had noticed that such "reversed cells" generated hydrogen at a much higher rate than usual. Unfortunately, these results weren't properly analyzed until a few days before the final test. Miller Hutchison knew about them, but he apparently didn't recognize their ominous significance. It was a fatal oversight.

Throughout Saturday morning, as the discharge phase of the

experiment progressed, Savvy prowled through the submarine checking and rechecking the fans, the temperature readings, the voltage and current levels. At noon he made a final inspection, climbed out through the main hatch, and walked the short distance to Dock Number Three, where the sub tender *Ozark* was moored, to have lunch with a friend. Before leaving he gave *E-Two*'s chief electrician, Henry Miles, specific instructions about monitoring and cooling the batteries.

Fourteen people remained in the submarine when Savvy left. In addition to Miles and his four electricians, nine plumbers from the Navy Yard were working on the high-pressure air tanks in the forward torpedo room.

The electricians had already begun watering the batteries, rolling up the waterproof canvas covering, opening the wooden shutters and methodically inserting a hose into each of the cells until enough water had been added. The procedure required about an hour's work for each compartment.

By 12:20 they had completed the forward compartment and were starting the rear one, but Electrician Second Class Ramon Otto was troubled. During the watering in the forward compartment, he'd noticed that the solution in the cells was unusually agitated. In some cases it was bubbling so violently that he couldn't read its level accurately.

Otto found a portable voltage meter and began measuring individual cells in the aft compartment. It didn't take him long to find two cells that had already reversed. He reported his findings to Chief Miles and then continued the watering process. This may have been the last opportunity anyone had to avert what was going to happen; but, in spite of the fact that it was exactly the kind of situation Savvy had warned him about, the chief electrician did nothing. Perhaps he'd been unduly influenced by Miller Hutchison's dismissal of the captain's warnings.

Shortly after 1:00 P.M. Otto carried an empty water barrel up to the deck to refill it. As he straddled the main hatch struggling to fit the barrel through the safety railing, there was a muffled thump and a huge force spun him into the air. On board the *Ozark,* Savvy Cooke heard the sound and felt a stab of alarm. Running to the window of the purser's office, he saw a puff of dirty white smoke rising above the *E-Two*'s main hatch. He hurried outside and joined the crowd rushing toward Dock Number Two.

By the time Savvy reached the sub, thick black smoke was billowing from all her hatches. The torpedo room hatch had been blown completely off the bow. Debris was scattered over the submarine's superstructure and the surrounding dock. To Savvy's horror the body of one of the *E-Two*'s electricians lay on the deck in a pool of blood, his right leg severed at the hip. The interior of the sub was an inferno. The explosion had ignited combustible material somewhere inside the hull and smoke and heat were pouring out.

Ignoring the danger Savvy led a group of men down through the main hatch. Inside they found a scene of devastation. Bodies were visible amid the rubble and the rescue party could hear men moaning and crying out for help, but they were unable to accomplish anything because of the dense fire and smoke.

Returning to the dock Savvy ordered fire hoses to be directed into the sub's interior. He found Ramon Otto wandering dazedly nearby. The space electrician's face was a singed mask and his arms were badly burned. After sending him to the hospital, Savvy ordered gas masks and fans to be brought and reentered the sub with another party of volunteers. Moving as quickly as possible through the shattered interior, the rescuers found a number of survivors, as well as several more bodies.

It was hard, dangerous work. Because of the heat and smoke they had to crawl along the deck. In some compartments the flooring had been blown up against the overhead and now lay in jumbled heaps, blocking the way. Bulkheads had been knocked down. Many of the dead and injured were covered by the rubble.

By 4:00 all the victims had been removed from the sub. The fire was out and the smoke had cleared. Savvy sat on the dock beside the *E-Two* and put his head in his hands. It had been a day from hell. Four men were dead and ten were injured, some of them seriously. Henry Miles and Ray Otto were in critical condition at Flushing Avenue Naval Hospital. Chief Miles had been discovered in the aft battery compartment, unconscious and badly burned. Both of his legs and one arm were fractured and it appeared that he had inhaled scalding gas. He wasn't expected to live. The other occupant of the aft compartment had been killed outright. Near the end of the day, a work party found the severed leg of the dead electrician, hidden under the ruined main switchboard.

The following day the commandant of the Navy Yard convened a board of investigation to probe the accident. Basing their conclusion on the deck plates and bulkheads that had been blown outward and on the burns on the inside of the battery well, the Board ruled that the explosion had been caused by hydrogen gas from the Edison Batteries. Rather than accept this verdict, Secretary Daniels ordered a formal court of inquiry. As a result during the ensuing weeks Savvy went through a second hell.

For a young officer a court of inquiry was a fearful thing, potentially ruinous of both career and reputation; officers had seen promising futures vanish for no better reason than the bad luck of being in the wrong place at the wrong time. There is perhaps no better example of this than the fate of Captain Charles Butler McVay, skipper of the cruiser, U.S.S. *Indianapolis,* which was sunk on July 30, 1945, by a Japanese submarine. McVay was court martialed and convicted in spite of compelling evidence that he was not culpable for the loss of his ship. His career in ruins, McVay eventually took his own life. He was only recently exonerated posthumously.

For Savvy Cooke the potential consequences were just as devastating. As the *E-Two*'s commanding officer, he was compelled to defend himself in the face of the hallowed naval tradition that a captain is ultimately responsible for everything that occurs on his ship, whether he knows about it or not.

To make matters worse, Miller Hutchison seemed to have forgotten his former good opinion of the *E-Two*'s captain. As the trial progressed, Edison's assistant went to ever greater lengths to shift responsibility for the accident onto Savvy's shoulders. At one point the engineer stated that the explosion had been caused by improper handling of the batteries by the submarine's electricians. He brought in an "expert" witness to prove from the color of the smoke that the explosion had not been caused by hydrogen and even went so far as to make comments to the press alleging overt carelessness by the sub's crew.

Hutchison's open hostility toward Savvy led to several heated exchanges in court. At one point the engineer was asked, "Did you ever tell Lieutenant Cooke that the reversed cells in an Edison storage battery generated gas to a greater extent than on normal discharge?"

"I did not consider it necessary," Hutchison replied, "any more than I would tell an engineer to keep water in his boiler. The batteries themselves were not any more to blame than is a steam boiler, when the water is withdrawn without first withdrawing the fire from the fire box."

It was an unfortunate comparison and it infuriated Savvy's friend and fellow officer Chester Nimitz, who was serving as defense counsel. Nimitz immediately subjected Hutchison to a volley of questions: "Are you acquainted with the phenomenon of boiler explosions? . . . Did you ever see a boiler explode? . . . Did you ever explode one by excessive pressures? . . . Did you ever hear of anybody that tried to explode one with excessive pressures?" and so forth, to each of which the increasingly flustered engineer had to answer "No."

At last Nimitz addressed the court, "The witness has expressed an opinion and the value of that opinion depends on how much the witness knows about boiler explosions. If the witness will admit that he does not know how steam boilers explode, I will have no objection to dropping this line of questioning."

The explosion at the Navy Yard and the subsequent hearings attracted widespread attention in the local press, which reported each day's testimony in great detail. From the beginning there was considerable sympathy for the young captain, who had repeatedly risked his life trying to save both his men and local workmen from the burning submarine. As additional facts in the case became known, public sentiment swung even further against the Edison Battery Company. A typical news report in the local paper described the court proceedings this way.

Until Lt. Cooke had told of writing to the Navy Department for a hydrogen detector to safeguard the men of the *E-2*, not a word had been said to indicate that any officer of the Navy or anybody else had ever had reason to foresee such an accident as overtook the *E-2*. Lt. Cooke, youthful in appearance, alert, and expert in matters pertaining to submarines, was the only witness before the court yesterday. He answered all questions in carefully measured words. It is doubtful if a clearer speaking witness ever appeared before a Naval court.

Public goodwill notwithstanding, day after day of testimony failed to produce the crucial evidence that Savvy needed. The men who could prove that he had done everything possible to prevent the explosion were either dead, or dying and unable to speak. His spirits weren't helped by the news that another injured crewman had passed away in the hospital, bringing the total number of dead to five. With Miles and Otto still in critical condition, that toll might rise still higher. It was Savvy's lowest point. With the proceedings nearing the end of their second week, the outcome seemed almost certain.

Then unexpectedly word came from the hospital that Chief Miles, who had hung on in spite of expectation, would be able to testify. Since the injured chief electrician couldn't leave his bed, the entire court made the journey to the hospital and convened at his bedside. The chief electrician told them about Savvy's numerous efforts to prevent the disaster and his careful inspection of the battery compartments on the day of the explosion. At the end of his testimony he described the reversed cells that Otto had brought to his attention and admitted that he himself had ignored Savvy's orders in failing to report them. When these revelations

1. Midshipman Charles Maynard Cooke Jr. in 1910.

2. The *S-Five* at sea. Visible in this view are the deck gun and the conning tower with the open bridge on its upper level. The eighteen-inch pipe for the main induction system runs on top of the pressure hull beneath the topside deck. The line of holes along the side are drainage ports for this space.

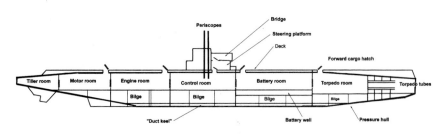

3. Schematic diagram of the *S-Five*.

4. Deck of an S-Boat looking aft from the bow. The widened area of the deck is for a gun emplacement. The portholes in the middle part of the conning tower show the location of the steering platform.

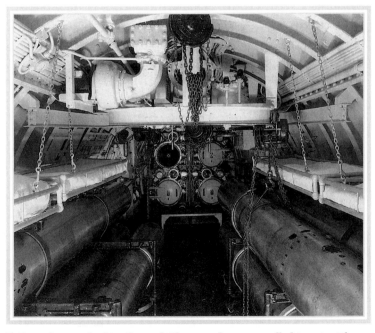

5. Torpedo room looking forward. The torpedoes are cradled in pairs. The overhead chain hoists and tracks are used to move the torpedoes. Several bunks are deployed. The torpedo launching tubes are the four circular hatches in the forward bulkhead (one of them open) surrounded by controls.

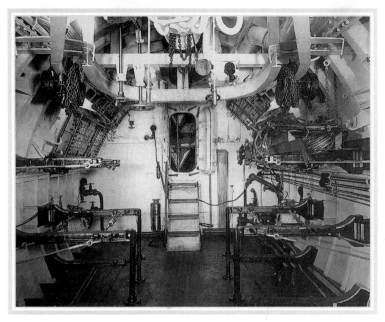

6. Torpedo room looking aft. The torpedo racks are empty in this view and the bunks are chained up. The port-side bilge valve that Henry Love opened is in the lower right of the photograph. The steps lead up to the battery room.

7. Battery room looking aft. At the far end of the compartment are the passageway and watertight door leading aft into the control room. Visible at the end of the compartment against the wall is one of the folding mess tables with the straps used by crewmen to escape from the flooded battery room.

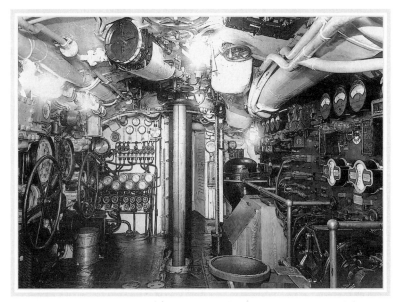

8. Control room looking forward. On the right side of the photograph is the main electrical switchboard where Chief Otto and Walter Nelson were stationed during the crash dive. The large white-faced gauges are current meters for the drive motors. The oblong boxes directly above each meter are the engine telegraphs labeled "Ahead," "Stop," "Back," and "Emergency." The large black kettle-shaped object is a gyroscopic compass (magnetic compasses will not work inside a sub's metal hull). The doorway leads to the battery room. The periscopes have been lowered. Left of center is the air manifold, where Chief Whitehead was stationed during the crash dive. Further left are the diving rudder controls, where Chief Fox had stationed himself just before flooding began. The large white pipe protruding from the overhead right of center is a ventilator outlet for the main induction system, the source of the flooding that sank the *S-Five*.

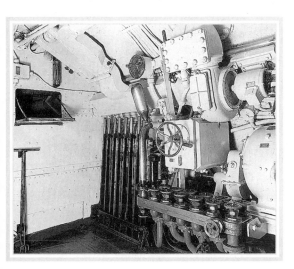

9. Control room looking aft, port side. The port Kingston control levers are near the center of the photograph. Note the hand-grip releases at the top of each lever and the locking bar at the bottom. The pass-through leads into the galley. The valves at the lower right are part of the bilge drainage system. The motor-driven centrifugal pump in the upper right may be the regulating pump, the only functioning pump on the *S-Five* after the sinking.

10. Engine room looking forward. The intake manifolds and paired rocker arms, which open and close the engine valves, are clearly visible. Crewmen used these to climb through the engine room after the sub was stood on her nose.

11. Tiller room viewed from the aft end of the motor room. The steering gears are visible inside the tiller room. This photograph gives a good view of the "dogging" levers used to seal the watertight door. Each lever extends through the bulkhead to a matching lever on the other side. Notice the pipe used for leverage to close the dogs tightly.

12. The stern of the *S-Five* with an unidentified ship, possibly the *Goethals*, in the background. The wooden scaffolding erected by Captain Johnson and his crew protrudes from the opposite (starboard) side of the sub.

13. The crew of the *S-Five* on the day after the rescue. Notice the bare feet, ragtag clothing, and blankets draped around shoulders.

Removed from the United States Submarine S–5, to allow the crew of that vessel to escape after being imprisoned 37 hours. The S–5 while engaged in diving exercises flooded a forward compartment and sank at 2.00 p.m. Sept.1,1920 in 165—feet of water. After repeated efforts the crew managed to bring the stern of the vessel to the surface, the vessel lying at an angle of 60° with the bow resting on the bottom. The crew managed to cut a small hole in the hull and by an improvised signal attracted the attention of a passing steamer, the ALANTHUS. Later the Pan—American steamer GEORGE W.GOETHALS arrived on the scene. The Chief Engineer of that vessel, Mr.W.G.Grace, assisted by the Chief Engineer of the Alanthus,Mr.C.Jacbsen working with a ratchet drill and chisel,removed this plate and at 3.00 a.m.Sept. 3,1920, the crew of the S—5 numbering 38 men were rescued

14. The plate removed from the *S-Five*'s hull during the rescue. The straight edge on the right side, which has been scored by hack saw cuts, is one edge of the smaller triangular hole cut by the submarine's crew.

were reported in the press, Edison withdrew his support for Hutchison and the trial was effectively over. At its official conclusion in mid-February, Savvy was absolved of any blame.

In spite of the hearing's favorable outcome, Savvy was deeply marked by the accident on the *E-Two*. He'd done everything he could to prevent disaster and yet men—his men—had died needlessly. For a military commander peacetime losses are often the hardest to bear. In the years that followed, Savvy would spend many sleepless nights, trying to accept what had happened. As if to add to his unhappiness, the Navy ignored his request for a return to sea duty and shipped him off to a land-locked supply ship anchored in Boston Harbor.

The local press took Savvy's side, but to no avail.

> Navy Yard officers are puzzled by the transfer of Lt. Charles M. Cooke Jr. from the submarine service to be engineering officer of the receiving ship Salem at the Boston Navy Yard. No official blame was placed on Lt. Cooke, according to the officers, who said the technical information he gave the Board of Inquiry about the disaster showed he was one of the best submarine officers in the Navy. . . . The young Lt. was badly shaken up over the accident and gave heroic service in rescuing several imprisoned men . . . and it was thought he would receive command of another submarine . . .

But Savvy wasn't given command of another sub. Instead, after a brief stint on the *Salem,* he was transferred to the Fore River Shipyard, a private company in nearby Quincy, where he would sit out the remainder of the war as an assistant inspector of machinery helping to build the submarines that other skippers would take into battle. Swallowing his disappointment in this "prosaic job," Savvy applied himself to his duties with his usual zeal, but he still hadn't given up hope of returning to sea. During his tour at Fore River, he subjected the Navy Department to a steady barrage of requests for combat duty. They were all denied.

Savvy's only consolation during this period was the birth of his first child on March 1, 1916, at Susina, the Georgia plantation at which Savvy and Leslie had honeymooned. They gave the little girl Leslie's maiden name, Temple. In the spring of 1916, shortly after his transfer to Fore River, Savvy was able to reunite with his wife and daughter, when Leslie moved up to Quincy. She and Temple settled into a small rented house in Wollaston, a beach-side community near the shipyard, and for the first time since their marriage the Cookes were able to live together as a couple.

It was not an idyllic period. Although Savvy had been able to visit Leslie immediately after Temple's birth, he'd been too in-volved with the Edison Battery and later with the court proceed-ings to spend time with her during the pregnancy. Although it might have been understandable in a practical sense, his absence hurt her deeply. Stung by her resentment, he became even more distant and their relationship deteriorated further. Nevertheless, in September Leslie announced that she was pregnant again. On June 2, 1917, she gave birth to their second daughter.

They named her Anne Bleecker, taking her middle name from Savvy's Dutch forebears on his mother's side, the same family that had given New York's famous Bleecker Street its name. Instead of strengthening the marriage, however, the new addition seemed only to add to the strain, with awful consequences.

Four months after the birth of their second daughter, on Octo-ber 17, Leslie killed herself. Her suicide was shocking and unex-pected, as such tragedies usually are, and in this case Savvy bore the added burden of feeling at least partially responsible. In re-strospect, it would be easy to blame marital difficulties and Savvy's long absences—as he did—but it's also quite possible that Leslie suffered from a severe case of postpartum depression, a diagnosis that was unknown at that time.

In spite of their differences, there's no doubt that Savvy cared deeply for Leslie. Her death was a devastating blow that would haunt him for years. On a more practical level, it left him with the difficult problem of pursuing a naval career while caring for two young children. It's not obvious what he would have done if his parents hadn't intervened. When Charles Senior learned about Leslie's death, he turned down the new job he'd been offered with the Internal Revenue Service and hurried north with his wife, Sarah, to look after their grandchildren. Savvy's parents stayed in Wollaston for a month, helping him to put his personal affairs in order, before taking Temple and Anne back to live with them in Fort Smith. Here was another agonizing choice for Savvy. He adored his children and would miss them terribly during the long intervals between visits, but he had no choice if he wished to remain a submarine captain.

In an effort to focus his attention away from Leslie's death, Savvy applied himself even more diligently to his work at the shipyard and redoubled his efforts to see action. In early 1918 his appeals were answered at last. His friend and former legal counsel, Chester Nimitz, who was now chief of staff to the commander of the Atlantic sub fleet, obtained an assignment for him as a naval observer in England. From May to June Savvy sailed on British submarines patrolling the North Sea from their base in the Orkney Islands. Although he saw little action during this period, he came back to the United States with a much better appreciation of British eccentricity and the clear impression that in the English Channel "the dangers from attacks from your own side were somewhat greater than attacks by the enemy!"

Following Savvy's return from England in the fall of 1918, things began to improve for him. After his eight years in the service, it came as no surprise when he made lieutenant, but the provisional promotion to lieutenant commander that followed several months later was an unexpected bonus. Finally in December his long exile from the sea came to an end. He received orders to take command of the *R-Two*, a new submarine that had just been completed at Fore River. His parents brought the girls up for the occasion and on January 24, 1919, with her husband and granddaughters watching proudly, Savvy's mother christened the new boat.

For the next eleven months Savvy commanded the *R-Two* in training missions along the east coast from her home port in New

London. In October 1919, he received orders to take command of yet another submarine, one of the new S-Class boats being developed at the Portsmouth Navy Yard. Thanks to his position at Fore River, Savvy was well informed about the latest events in the submarine program. This was an important assignment and he knew it.

In December, after spending Christmas in Arkansas with his parents and the girls, he boarded the train for Portsmouth.

# 8

## SECOND WIND

"Sad patience, too near neighbor to despair."
— MATTHEW ARNOLD

WEDNESDAY, 19:00—CONTROL ROOM.

Seven years in the undersea service had changed the way Charlie
Grisham thought about submarines. As a junior enlisted man
working his way up through the ratings, he'd regarded them as little more than cold impersonal shells filled with machinery; but as
time passed, he became aware of things he'd overlooked: things
like the photographs and letters taped to locker doors, the tattered books and dog-eared playing cards tucked under mattresses, harmonicas, toothbrushes, pocket knives, clothing hung
up to dry . . . in short, the rich tapestry of everyday living aboard
subs that softened their hard angularity and gave each of them
character and individuality.

Looking around at the jumbled ruin that had been the *S-Five*'s
command center, he marveled at how swiftly and completely that
human veneer could be stripped away, leaving only gleaming steel
and heaps of sodden wreckage looking chilly and alien in the light
from the crippled electrical system.

The boat sounded different, too. Gone was the reassuring

throb of propellers that had so often lulled Charlie to sleep on patrol. In its place was an eerie quiet, punctuated by the muted
plunk of dripping water and abrupt creaking and groaning noises
that came intermittently from the *S-Five*'s tortured hull.

On every side tired, battered crewmen clung to the sides of the
compartment, trying vainly to rest, but it was nearly impossible for
anyone to find a comfortable position. Each man had to hang on to
something at all times or risk sliding down into the nauseating
sump in the forward end of the control room. Even the simplest
movement required great care, because everything in the sub was
slippery.

There was little conversation. Savvy had instructed the crew to
remain as quiet as possible in order to conserve oxygen. Huddled
silently with their arms wrapped around themselves for warmth,
the men resembled a family of bats dangling along the margins of
a long, narrow cave.

Luckily the air quality had held up reasonably well. Charlie
could tell that he was breathing faster than usual, but he didn't
feel uncomfortable. Indeed, the major problem with breathing
was the smell. To put it bluntly, the *S-Five* stank! True, no submarine smelled good. Even in ideal conditions the odor of close-
packed men who could rarely shower or wash clothing mixed with
the taint of motor oil, diesel exhaust, and stagnant water to make a
ripe atmosphere in any sub, and conditions in the *S-Five* were far
from ideal. By stirring up the depths of the bilges, the flooding had
produced a truly breathtaking stench, which was accentuated by
the lack of a functioning toilet. The fact that no one had joked
about the odor was an indication of how truly oppressive it was.
Few things were beyond humor in a submarine!

At least the astringent traces of chlorine had faded, now that
the battery room had been sealed, but Charlie knew it was only a
matter of time until the gas reappeared. He pictured it creeping
inexorably toward them through the bulkhead, seeping through
gaskets, worming its way along wiring bundles. Like the flooding
and the dwindling air supply, the gas had become another uncon-
trollable factor in their mortal countdown.

Not far from Charlie, John Longstaff had kept up his watch at the depth gauge. From sixty-two feet, when he'd started keeping track an hour ago, the reading had climbed to fifty-three feet. This was a respectable increase, but the changes weren't coming as frequently now, and Charlie knew why. The gain in height had come entirely from standing the *S-Five* up straighter, while her bow remained firmly planted on the sea floor. If they continued this process, the *S-Five* would eventually be straight up and down. What if that was all they could do? What would it mean? The numbers were tantalizing, almost mockingly close. The *S-Five* was 231 feet long. If the sub were vertical in 180 feet of water, then the sub would project *fifty-one* feet out of the water. And the motor room hatch was *fifty-two* feet from the stern!

So, even if reality precisely matched the figures, the motor room hatch would still lie one foot (one lousy foot!) beneath the surface and they *still* wouldn't be able to open it without sinking the *S-Five*.

Of course, reality might *not* be ideal. The actual depth of the sea here might be slightly greater or less than 180 feet. The sub's gauges might be off. *Any* of these circumstances could make escape either more or less likely.

Charlie agreed with the Captain: the only way for them to escape was to get the sub's bow off the bottom; and that meant getting rid of the water in the torpedo room.

Could they do that? Maybe. The regulating pump had reached its limit in the torpedo room an hour and a half ago, when the water level in that compartment dropped below the aft bilge intake. That left only Savvy's technique of forcing water back through the induction system using compressed air. As long as that continued to work they had a chance, but their reserve of compressed air was steadily decreasing. Charlie worried that it would be exhausted before the sub lifted off the bottom.

He hadn't considered the possibility that something *else* might go wrong. So when word was passed down from the steering platform that bubbles were rising past the eye ports, he experienced a distinctly queasy feeling. Those bubbles could have only one source: the torpedo room. But what did they mean? Charlie wasn't surprised when Savvy asked him to climb up and see what *kind* of bubbles they were.

For submarines bubbles came in two varieties. "Water bubbles" were the small round specks that formed when turbulent flow dislodged bits of air from the seams in pipes and valves. They were innocuous. "Air bubbles," on the other hand, were large and flat-bottomed, and could only form when sizable amounts of air entered the system. That would mean trouble.

On his way to the conning tower ladder Charlie recognized the *S-Five*'s newest crewman, a young second-class seaman who had recently come over from the flotilla's sub tender, *Rainbow*.

"What d'you think of submarine life so far?" Charlie asked facetiously as he climbed past.

"I'd rather be back on the *Rainbow*, Sir!" the sailor assured him without smiling.

Bad joke, Charlie decided, as he continued up the ladder and crawled through the hatch onto the steering platform. Threading his way between the tightly packed men, he peered through one porthole after another, until he found the bubbles. He didn't have to look long; they were big and flat. With a sigh he crawled back to the hatch and lowered himself onto the ladder. Perhaps he was preoccupied by what he'd just seen. Perhaps he was simply tired. In any event, as he ducked under the hatch, he made an uncharacteristic mistake and allowed the lanyard to loop around his neck, pulling the hatch cover down onto his head.

Unlike the outer hatch, the inner one wasn't held open by a spring. Only the fact that Charlie's hands were above his shoulders at the time saved him from a nasty injury. As it was, the hatch cover gave him a painful rap and pinned his head against the rim. For a moment he lost his temper. "Get this damned hatch off my head!" he growled at no one in particular.

George Bill, the gunner's mate who'd been at the helm during the dive, was already scrambling over to help. Lifting the hatch off the exec's head, he held it up while another sailor wedged it open.

Charlie climbed down from the conning tower under his own power. When they heard him speak a few minutes later, the sailors concluded that he was okay. Charlie subsequently discovered a large contusion on the side of his scalp, but by that time he had more urgent things to worry about.

Savvy appeared to take the news about the bubbles calmly, but in reality he was bitterly disappointed. If air was being forced out through the induction system, it could only mean that the water level in the torpedo room had fallen below the ventilator outlet, and that effectively put an end to his trick with the compressed air. To continue would merely waste their remaining supply. He told Fred Whitehead to stop pressurizing the torpedo room. Then he slid down onto the bulkhead beside Charlie Grisham to discuss their remaining options.

The problem was, there were no other options, now that Savvy's last method for emptying the torpedo room had failed.

In other words they were going to die.

This left Savvy with one last difficult decision: how to break the news to the crew. As long as there'd been a possibility of escape, he'd held back the most brutal realities of their situation, but the air bubbles signified an end to that. He couldn't let these brave young men go on dreaming about seeing their families, their wives, their sweethearts, when it wasn't going to happen. Before long their real suffering would begin, and he owed them the ability to meet it with honesty and dignity.

While Savvy tried to find the right words, Charlie Grisham climbed up to the speaking tubes to talk with Bill Bender. A few minutes later he was back and he was excited. According to Bender, he and Reb Hutson had climbed up into the motor room, where they'd heard waves lapping against the hull!

Waves breaking against the hull? The statement jarred Savvy's thinking. Until now he'd been focused on escaping through one of the sub's hatches, but that was now out of the question, and suddenly he found himself considering a possibility that would not have occurred to him before.

Much depended upon what Bender and Hutson had actually heard. Sound sometimes did peculiar things in water. Submariners were accustomed to hearing noises transmitted down from the surface: the churning of propellers, the blaring of radios, even the rattling of dishes in the galleys of ships passing overhead.

Was that the case here, or had the two chiefs actually heard waves smacking directly against the *S-Five*'s hull? Savvy would have liked nothing better than to run up to the motor room and listen for himself, but the engine room door was still covered by nearly two feet of water. Perhaps there was another way to determine the truth.

Savvy summoned John Longstaff down from the depth gauge and told him to bring his screwdriver with him. Using it they unfastened an inclinometer from its position over the diving rudder controls. Like a carpenter's level, an inclinometer showed the sub's angle relative to horizontal using an air bubble in a glass arc. They positioned the gauge on a nearby bulkhead so that the bubble was centered. Then they drew two lines, one horizontal according to the inclinometer and the other parallel to the hull. The angle between these lines measured just over fifty-seven degrees. A little trigonometry gave them their answer. If the bottom was really at 180 feet, then the last fourteen feet of the *S-Five*'s stern should be above the surface.

Until now Savvy had been in no hurry to reach the stern. The sailors back there seemed to be doing well enough under Hutson and Bender. Savvy had seen no reason to risk injury to his crew by asking them to force the engine room door. Eventually the regulating pump would eliminate the pool of water blocking it.

Chief Bender's news about the motor room changed all that.

They started a few minutes later. With Savvy and Fox pushing from below and Bender's men hauling on a pry bar from above, the engine room door lifted a fraction of an inch. A thin sheet of water jetted through the crack, drenching the sailors below. Like everything in the sub, the water was contaminated with oil, which made things distinctly more difficult for Savvy and Fox, but they shook the nasty stuff out of their eyes and continued pushing. The crack gradually widened and presently, after several tons of water and oil had passed through, the door lifted without resistance. The way to the stern was clear.

Savvy chose Fred Whitehead to accompany him to the stern. The rest of the men, including Ensign Longstaff and Chief Otto, would remain in the control room under Lieutenant Grisham's command. Their primary responsibility would be to cycle the regulating pump from one bilge to another and to pressurize the torpedo room periodically to drive the water level back down. Savvy would have preferred keeping pressure on the torpedo room continuously to prevent the leak occurring at all, but the last air bank was down to 400 p.s.i., and he wanted to hold some of that air in reserve.

Before leaving the control room, Savvy gave the men a short pep talk, reviewing things they needed to remember: staying calm, moving around as little as possible, conserving oxygen. Grisham appreciated the gesture. The men had such faith in the captain that a word from him made discipline much easier to maintain. The last thing Savvy said before climbing into the engine room was, "I'm sorry to tell you this, boys, but the smoking lamp is *not* lit!" It got a good laugh.

### 19:30—Control Room.

Grisham watched the captain and Whitehead disappear through the aft bulkhead. The door closed behind them. Considering all the effort they'd expended to open that door, it seemed a shame to close it again. An open door would have facilitated communication and improved the men's spirits, but it would also have allowed any chlorine gas that reached the control room to contaminate the rest of the sub. Charlie shrugged his shoulders fatalistically. He was more interested in why Savvy was in such a hurry to get to the stern.

Although the captain hadn't confided in him, Charlie was sure he knew what Savvy had in mind. It couldn't involve the motor room hatch, which was still too far underwater. That left only one possibility: Savvy intended to cut through the hull where it protruded from the sea. And if that was his purpose, Charlie understood why he'd kept it to himself. The *S-Five* carried only a few hand tools and these weren't at all well-suited to cutting though metal, let alone three-fourths-inch of high-strength steel.

In Charlie's opinion the captain intended to try his plan before revealing it to the crew. Watching yet another scheme fail—even at this late hour—could only harm morale. Charlie had already noticed that Savvy encouraged the men to put their faith in him, rather than in any particular strategy. The technique seemed to work. Charlie remembered one of the sailors pointing out that the captain "didn't look excited any," when he climbed up through the engine room door. Nearby crewmen had nodded approvingly. As long as the captain appeared confident, it seemed to be enough for them. It was valuable lesson in command. Assuming he lived long enough to profit from it.

Time passed slowly in the control room. Shifting the regulating pump from one bilge to another and cycling the main induction valve didn't require much effort, except when the pump ran hot and they had to shut it down and comb the compartment for grease to lubricate it. In general the men seemed content to rest, probably, Charlie thought, because they felt as sick as he did. The air was becoming extremely bad. At one point John Longstaff climbed into a corner, bent over and began quietly vomiting. He wasn't the first. The reek of vomit and human waste had become a ghastly presence in the air around them.

Grisham found himself staring at the barometer. The air pressure in the control room had risen steadily, driven up by leakage through the air manifold and compression by the flooding. Finally the gauge's needle had "pegged" itself at the top of the scale; but, if Charlie was right about the captain's purpose, it wouldn't stay there. The moment a drill broke through the hull, air would begin pouring out and the pressure inside the sub would fall. Eventually it would register on the barometer.

It was frustrating. If the *S-Five*'s stern was out of the water, her crew was literally an inch away from safety; but without a cutting torch or power tools, that inch might as well be a mile. It was another of the countless tradeoffs due to lack of space in subs. Heavy equipment wasn't needed often enough to justify carrying it. In the rare instances when submarines suffered major damage but didn't sink, they limped back to the nearest port as best they could. A case in point was submarine *R-Fourteen*, which lost all mechanical and electrical power in mid-Pacific on May 10, 1921, and spent five days *sailing* back to Hawaii using her periscope as a mast.

Perhaps it was just as well that Charlie couldn't know about the *S-Fourteen*. As it was, he became so absorbed in his thoughts that he missed what he was waiting to see. The next time he looked at the barometer, its needle was hovering above the stop pin. So, it had happened: the captain had made a hole in the side of the boat! Grisham was consumed by curiosity. Had Savvy managed to get through to open air or had he merely created another leak? The executive officer stared impatiently at the closed engine room door and waited.

## 20:00—Motor Room.

It took longer than Savvy had expected to reach the stern. Clambering over the diesels in the engine room was relatively easy, because the rows of parallel rocker arms formed a convenient ladder; but by the time Savvy and Whitehead reached the door to the motor room, they were breathing heavily and their legs were trembling. Ordinarily the climb shouldn't have been taxing. It was a sign that the air was getting worse.

After catching their breath, they continued. Climbing was more difficult in the motor room and the danger of falling greater, but by moving slowly and carefully they reached the stern safely. Hutson and Bender were waiting for them beneath the tiller room bulkhead. This bulkhead was smaller than the others in the sub, because the hull had begun to taper here. The large wheel protruding from its starboard side was the aft or "emergency" helm, used to guide the boat if the linkage to the conning tower failed.

Bender had been right: the sound of waves slapping against the hull was unmistakable; but exactly how high did the water reach outside? For several minutes Savvy and the chiefs spread out through the motor room, trying to determine this without success. Eventually, Savvy decided that the safest course was to drill through the hull as far back in the stern as he could reach. He ordered Hutson and Bender to open the tiller room, while Whitehead went to procure a drill and some metal-boring bits. Finding anything useful in the snarl of material left by the flood seemed like an impossible task, but Bender seemed confident he could come up with something. By the time the tiller room door was open, he was back with a breast drill and a small assortment of bits.

Someone on the S-Five once described the tiller room as "about the size of a doghouse." It was actually bigger than that, but not by much. Two pairs of linked steering gears, each more than a foot in diameter, occupied the center of the wedge-shaped chamber, leaving very little room around them, but by contorting themselves into uncomfortable positions, Savvy and Bender managed to squeeze inside.

Bender inserted a quarter-inch bit into the breast drill and tightened the chuck. Turning his body sideways and edging as far back into the stern as possible, he set the bit against the hull and began turning the hand crank. The position was awkward and the bit had an annoying tendency to skitter sideways on the smooth surface, but, with Savvy steadying him, Bender stuck with it. Soon a trail of silvery flakes was sifting down the hull beneath him.

The breast drill resembled a standard woodworker's drill with a padded butt. By placing this against shoulder or chest the user could apply his weight to the drill, while using his hands to turn the crank around. For drilling straight down, the arrangement worked nicely, but it wasn't well suited for working horizontally, and it was next to useless for drilling upward. Although it wasn't ideal for what Savvy had in mind, it would have to do for the time being. They could look for additional tools, once they had a better idea of what they were up against.

After drilling for what seemed like a long time, Bender stopped and pulled the bit aside. He and Savvy bent to examine the shallow conical pit he'd made, while Hutson and Whitehead craned to see from outside the door. It was obvious that cutting through the hull was going to be harder than they'd expected. Wordlessly Bender replaced the bit in the hole and began turning the hand crank again. This time he didn't stop until the drill broke through. Breathing heavily he began backing the drill out until it pulled free, leaving a small dark hole. No water flowed in, and when Savvy put his ear to it, he could hear the whisper of escaping air. They'd done it!

With some difficulty Savvy maneuvered himself to look through the little drill hole, but he could see only darkness. Then he remembered to check his watch. It was 8:30 in the evening. The sun had been down for two hours and the moon had just come up, so he wasn't surprised that he couldn't see anything. Nevertheless, the lack of visibility deprived him of a key piece of information, because he couldn't tell how far their test hole was above the surface. It might be several feet or several inches, in which case their proposed escape route might be swamped by waves at any time.

Then he had an idea. Straightening from his awkward crouch, he called out to Hutson and asked him to climb down to the crew's head and open the flood valves. A few minutes later the chief returned to report that the valves were dry. Savvy was satisfied. The crew's head was nearly ten feet further forward. That was a large enough margin. He proceeded to outline the plan of attack. Starting with the test hole they would continue drilling until they had outlined an opening large enough for a man to squeeze through. Savvy would return to the control room to organize the crew into working parties to help with the drilling.

As he spoke, Savvy was aware of the difficulties they faced.

Hampered by the awkward position he'd been forced to assume, Chief Bender had taken nearly twenty minutes to drill that first hole, and he was one of the strongest members of the crew. By even the most conservative estimate, using the largest bits they had, it would require more than 100 holes to accomplish their goal. Using Bender's time, that represented at least thirty hours of non-stop drilling, without even taking into account other obstacles and delays. Thirty hours! Would their meager supply of tools last that long? Would the air? Or the men themselves? Whitehead and Bender must have understood the problems, but they listened attentively while Savvy gave them their orders, and then set to work as if they hadn't the slightest doubt of success.

### 20:35—Control Room.

Savvy made his way back down through the sub. Descending was easier, but still strenuous. He could see that moving men up and down in the tilted sub might become a significant problem, particularly as the air got worse. Stopping briefly in the engine room, he sent more men aft, including Walter Nelson, the electrician who had forced his way up against the flooding to close the engine room door. Somewhere in the *S-Five* there was an electric drill. If Nelson could find it and make it run, the work would go much more quickly.

According to Grisham, things had gone well in the control room during Savvy's absence. The exec did remark that the air was becoming foul, but Savvy had noticed that the moment he entered the control room. The crew couldn't stay there much longer, but Savvy didn't want to give up the control room before it became absolutely necessary. He told Grisham to stick it out as long as possible.

When he was ready to head back to the stern, Savvy addressed the crew again, but this time he told them about the possibility of an escape route. "We have a fighting chance now, boys!" he assured them. With Grisham's assistance, he picked several additional men to accompany him aft. Percy Fox was one of them. After his terrible oversight during the crash dive, the big chief petty officer had been eager to help in any way he could.

As the little group started up through the sub, Savvy was struck by something. As far as he knew, not once in all the long frightful hours since the accident had a single member of the crew criticized Fox for his mistake.

# 9

# DRILLING

"Ah, but a man's reach should exceed his grasp, or what's
a Heaven for?"

— ROBERT BROWNING

## WEDNESDAY, 21:00—TILLER ROOM.

In the half hour it took Savvy to descend to the control room and
return, Bender and Whitehead had drilled a second hole and
were beginning the third. Using a five-eighths-inch-diameter bit,
the largest they could find, they were spacing the holes less than
an inch apart. When they had carved out the triangular metal tabs
that were left, using the hammer and chisel that Whitehead had
found, the result was an irregular slot about as wide as a fingertip
and just over an inch long.

By the time Savvy pulled himself through the doorway into the
tiller room, both Bender and Whitehead were nearly exhausted.
Yet they were vigorous men. It was an indication of how debili-
tated everyone in the *S-Five* had become, worn down by fatigue,
lack of food and water, and bad air. If the drilling was to continue
without interruption, their manpower would have to be managed
carefully.

Savvy ordered Walter Nelson to join the two chiefs. Then he
began organizing the remaining men into groups of three, includ-

ing an officer to be responsible for each team's readiness. By 9:30 the drillers were hard at work. Their first goal was to extend the slot that Bender and Whitehead had begun until it was large enough to accommodate a hacksaw. Savvy believed that cutting through the hull with a saw would go faster than nibbling at it with drills and chisels.

From the beginning the work was tedious and uncomfortable. Three people could squeeze into the tiller room—barely—but only two could actually get near the hole at one time. Usually these two would operate the breast drill for as long as they could and then rest, while the third member of the team knocked out the metal tabs. The entire process required between twenty and thirty minutes of work for each hole—hard, awkward toil that left arms and shoulders aching, hands blistered and raw. To add to these troubles their tools, which had never been intended for such demanding duty, broke down repeatedly. Drill bits and chisels became dull and had to be sharpened. The breast drill's hand crank loosened and had to be tightened. Sometimes it seemed that they spent as much time repairing the tools as they did enlarging the escape hole. As soon as he could spare them, Savvy sent several men to scour the sub for additional implements: drill bits, files, hammers, hacksaw blades, and chisels, "anything that will cut steel!"

During his first shift with Chief Whitehead, Walter Nelson watched the chief engineer struggle with the breast drill. Then he climbed down into the motor room and returned a few minutes later carrying a length of broom handle.

"It's a lever," he explained in response to Whitehead's quizzical look. The idea was to amplify the pressure on the drill with it. Whitehead agreed that Nelson had a nice theory, but in his opinion it didn't accomplish much in practice. When the Captain called Nelson out of the tiller room somewhat later to work with the electric drill, Whitehead promptly discarded the broom handle. Nevertheless the attempt had suggested another possibility to him. "Why don't we use an Old Man?" he proposed.

It was a good idea, Savvy agreed, and since Whitehead had thought of it, *he* could set it up.

An "Old Man" was a short, sturdy billet of wood with pulleys attached at one end. Torpedo men used it to load their huge "fishes." By passing ropes from the sides of the torpedo tube through the pulleys at one end and heaving on the ropes, they could drive the other end against the torpedo and shove it deep into the launching tube. Fred thought the same device might help them to force the unwieldy breast drill against the hull.

Locating an Old Man wasn't difficult, Whitehead discovered, but getting his hands on it proved to be a real struggle. Savvy and the others could hear him swearing and tossing equipment around as he dug it out from under "all the heavy things on the ship," but the effort proved to be worthwhile. When they had fastened the Old Man to the drill, threaded lines through the pulleys, and pulled them up tight, the work progressed noticeably faster.

After Nelson had recovered from his shift in the tiller room, Savvy sent him to find the electric drill. Once again the search was the easy part. Getting the device to work taxed Nelson's ingenuity and patience. Power tools circa 1920 weren't designed with the double-insulated plastic construction that makes modern equipment so durable and safe. The *S-Five*'s drill was made entirely out of metal, and the flooding had filled it with seawater and grounded its electric motor. To get current to it in the first place, Nelson had to disassemble two portable searchlights and splice their power cables together. He connected the resulting line to the sub's lighting circuit, which was their only remaining source of electricity. When he turned the drill on, it promptly short-circuited and blew all the fuses in the system.

Fumbling in the dim glow of the emergency lights, Nelson put in new fuses, then took the drill apart, dried each component as thoroughly as he could, and reassembled it. Wrapping rags around the handles to provide extra insulation, he flipped the power switch again. This time the short circuit current wasn't enough to blow the fuses, but it passed easily through the metal casing and the damp rags into Nelson, whose wet clothing made him an excellent conductor. The shock made his muscles spasm and clamped his hands onto the drill so firmly that he couldn't let go.

With his face set in an agonized rictus, the electrician tried valiantly to push the drill up against the hull, but his arms were fixed rigidly at his sides by the muscle contractions. After nearly a minute of this futile torture, a fuse blew and Walter slumped against the bulkhead. The drill went clattering into a corner of the tiller room. As the electrician rubbed his aching forearms, Savvy laughed and clapped him on the shoulder. It had been a nice try; the captain assured him; maybe he should use more rags next time. The shipper was right. The electric drill was too valuable a tool to abandon without a fight. Nelson took it apart, dried the insides and patiently put it back together again. This time the current leak was . . . tolerable.

It was nearly 10:30 P.M. by the time they got the electric drill working. The manual drilling teams had been hard at it for an hour with little enough to show for their effort. The slot that Bender and Whitehead had begun was now an inch and a half long and three-quarters of an inch wide. For the next half hour the men in the drilling teams uncomplainingly took turns, bracing their wet backs against the metal hull, gripping the damp drill handles in both hands and enduring electrical shocks that knotted their muscles and made their faces twitch with pain. The other members of their teams held them in place and kept the drill bit aligned. Fuses still blew occasionally, and each time Walter Nelson dutifully replaced them. In the meantime, he handed up tools whenever other workmen called for them. Painful though it was, the electric drill bored through the hull with gratifying speed.

## 21:00—Control Room.

After the Captain left the control room for the second time, Charlie Grisham found waiting even harder to endure. He tried to imagine what was going on in the stern. How many holes had been drilled? And where? More important, how many *remained* to be drilled? The routines of shifting and maintaining the regulating pump and cycling the pressure on the main induction system weren't demanding enough to take Charlie's mind off these questions. But shortly before nine o'clock something did. Charlie smelled chlorine gas.

It wasn't hard to identify the odor; any homemaker would recognize it immediately as the familiar smell of household bleach. Charlie had been expecting it. The drill holes in the stern would allow the air to escape and lower the air pressure in the stern compartments. The higher pressure inside the battery room would then drive chlorine gas toward the control room more rapidly. It wouldn't be long until one of the other sailors noticed the smell, but until then, Charlie decided not to mention it.

The exec understood the effects of chlorine well enough, having studied it during submarine school. It was a potent poison. The Germans had demonstrated that in France during the war. (In fact it was the first poison gas actually used in combat.) When it entered the respiratory system, it combined with water to form hydrochloric acid. Brief exposure caused irritation of the eyes, nose, and throat, while higher concentrations caused tissue damage and swelling. Ultimately the lungs began to fill with fluid, leading to the slow suffocation that was the principal cause of death, unless heart failure carried the victim off sooner. Charlie smiled dolefully. Drowning, oxygen starvation, carbon dioxide poisoning. Now they could add chlorine gas toxicity to the list of interesting ways to die.

The fact that Charlie could smell the chlorine meant that it had reached a concentration of about one part per million in the control room. From what Charlie had learned, when it reached two or three times that level, people would start coughing and sneezing. As if they could read his thoughts, several crewmen spoke up to ask about chlorine gas. They knew that the battery room had been flooded.

Thinking of what the captain would do in this type of situation, Charlie gave a little speech about the gas and its effects, but neglected the most gruesome details. At the end he declared, "Boys, if it does make its appearance in our midst, we'll have lots of time to abandon the room before it becomes strong enough to do any damage."

The lecture seemed to satisfy everyone, but it didn't buy Charlie much time. Soon after he finished speaking a sailor began to cough. Before long it seemed to Charlie that the whole world was sneezing in his face. By 9:15 conditions in the control room had become excruciating. Men were gasping, their faces contorted from the burning in their noses and throats. Tears ran down their cheeks from bloodshot eyes and the sound of wheezing filled the compartment with a shrill whistling noise.

When Charlie called to inform the captain, Savvy suggested that they put on gas masks and stay longer, but a hurried count showed there weren't enough masks. In the conning tower alone there were only two masks for half a dozen sailors. Besides, the activated charcoal filters in the gas masks would do nothing about low oxygen and high carbon dioxide levels. Grudgingly Savvy gave the order to evacuate the control room, but he didn't want Charlie and his men to leave empty-handed. He told them to bring water, signal lamps, batteries, and anything else that might be useful.

The water was a good idea, if they could find a way to carry it. Eventually one of the sailors dug two buckets from under the sink in the galley. "But they're 'slop' buckets," he reported doubtfully, referring to their normal use for carrying garbage.

"Wipe 'em out and fill 'em anyway," Charlie told him, "That water will taste sweet later on, no matter what kind of bucket it comes in!"

He and Percy Fox had been trying to find a battery for the sub's Aldis lamp, a powerful handheld light with a shutter that allowed it to send Morse Code. If they escaped from the sub at night, the lamp might be useful in a number of ways. Fox found a battery, but it was firmly fastened near the conning tower ladder and, like nearly everything else in the sub, it was wet and oily. After a long struggle, during which both men received numerous unpleasant shocks, they succeeded in unbolting it.

"Well, that surely did shake us up a bit, didn't it?" Charlie joked, as he watched the Chief wipe grime from the battery with a rag. Then he noticed the Chief's glum expression.

"What's wrong?" he asked.

Fox held the battery up to the light, so that Charlie could read the label. It was a battery for the gyrocompass motors!

One of the electricians, who was standing nearby said, "That's all right, sir. I can find the right one for you!" A few minutes later he returned with the correct battery. Charlie inserted it into the lamp, screwed down the contacts, and turned on the switch. Nothing! The lamp was broken.

Savvy's last order had been for someone to connect the air manifold to a service line leading aft, so that they could use the remaining compressed air without returning to the control room. While Ramon Otto took care of that task, Charlie sent a man to fetch George Bill and the other sailors down from the steering platform. When everyone was present and accounted for, Frank Peters climbed up to open the engine room door. Water had accumulated on top of it again, but after one of the other sailors had climbed up to help, they got it open. The usual rain of water and oil soaked everyone for a third time, but no one really cared. They just wanted to see the last of the control room. As Peters put it, no one was backward about getting out.

It was a 9:45 when they finished evacuating the control room. By this time the crew of the *S-Five* had been underwater for eight hours, for five of which Grisham and his men had held things together in the control room. After closing the watertight door and dogging it shut, Charlie sat down on the bulkhead beside Percy Fox and John Longstaff. Compared to the horrible atmosphere in the control room, the air here in the engine room was cool and refreshing. Charlie was bone weary and his throat was sore from all the talking he'd done in that caustic environment.

Longstaff must have been tired, too, because he promptly fell asleep, sprawled across the watertight door and snoring gently. Charlie and Chief Fox watched the rest of the crew disperse through the compartment hunting for comfortable spots. These were hard to come by; although the engine room was large, it was packed with machinery. The diesels alone occupied most of the available space. Consequently the majority of the men continued climbing through the aft doorway into the motor room.

George Bill was about to follow his shipmates into the stern, but he stopped when he reached the motor room bulkhead. Bill's clothing was soaked through from the latest drenching in the control room, and he was shaking from cold and fatigue. The climb from the control room had winded him to such a degree, it seemed as though the ship had grown several times longer since the last time he'd come this way. Pausing at the upper end of the compartment, he put his hand on the starboard diesel to steady himself. To his surprise the metal still retained a substantial amount of heat. Bill abandoned his original intention, draped himself across the engine block and dozed off immediately, oblivious to the sharp angles and bolt heads digging into his ribs.

Frank Peters kept climbing until he reached the tiller room door. Here he found his friend Walter Nelson blearily tending the lighting circuit that was providing power to the electric drill.

"Let me take over for you, Nels," Peters said, gently moving the other electrician aside. Nelson didn't resist. Instead he lowered himself slowly down to the crew's washroom, which offered several precious horizontal surfaces. Not surprisingly these were already occupied, but after tactful negotiation, Nelson was able to find space for himself. Not long after he'd wedged himself in, he heard another exhausted voice ask, "Room for one more, Nels?"

"Oh, yes," Nelson said with a resigned sigh. He squeezed sideways. "Always room for one more!" By the time the newcomer had piled on, Nelson was fast asleep.

23:15—Tiller Room.

The electric drill failed after completing half a dozen holes. By this time Frank Peters estimated that he'd replaced more than two dozen fuses to keep it going. Chief Otto came up from the control room to help. The chief didn't agree with Frank's pessimistic assessment of the drill, so he broke it down and began drying its components one more time.

But Nelson had been right: in spite of Chief Otto's ministrations, the electric drill was dead. Otto theorized that the voltage from the flooded batteries had fallen too low to operate it. Whatever the reason, the trapped sailors now had only the hand-powered breast drill, which seemed by comparison to make snail-like progress. As if to compensate, one of the crewmen uncovered a ratchet drill.

Unlike the breast drill, which required an awkward turning motion to rotate the bit, the ratchet drill employed a side-mounted lever, connected to the bit through a set of beveled gears. Besides offering a tremendous mechanical advantage, the ratchet could be operated with a more comfortable back and forth movement. The ratchet drill was a timely discovery for another reason; the breast drill had nearly worn out. "A life-saver," Chief Bender exclaimed when he saw the new tool.

By 10:00 P.M. the hole had grown large enough to look through, but it was dark outside and those who attempted to see were uniformly disappointed. As far as anyone could tell, there wasn't a star in the sky. Even more worrisome, the moon, which was only two days past full, was nowhere to be seen. Some of the men speculated that the sky might be overcast, which suggested the frightening possibility that the weather might turn bad. A storm, even a mild blow-up, might send the sub back to the bottom.

It would have been nice if the risk had been balanced by gain; but, contrary to expectation, the gap in the hull hadn't improved the air inside the sub. The men who worked in the tiller room could press their faces against the hole and snatch a few tantalizing breaths, but otherwise the heat and high pressure inside the sub prevented fresh air from flowing in.

23:15—Engine Room.

After he'd spent an hour and a half slumped on the engine room bulkhead, time began to drag along rather slowly for Charlie

Grisham. Fox and Longstaff were asleep next to him. The rest of the crew had disappeared into the motor room. So he was happy when the captain sent word for him to come up to the tiller room. At last he'd get to see how much progress had been made, maybe even lend a hand at the drilling himself.

As he climbed up through the gloom, the S-Five's exec had to move slowly and place his feet carefully so as not to step on anyone. When he finally poked his head into the tiller room, his first impression was how astonishing it was that three grown men could pack themselves into the tiller room, much less accomplish anything there.

Charlie wriggled through the doorway and squirmed around the steering gears into the starboard side of the little chamber. Now that he could see what they'd been doing, Charlie wasn't impressed. About midway between the deck and the overhead and a little more than halfway toward the aft end of the compartment, a small vertical slot about three inches long and three quarters of an inch wide had been carved through the hull, modest progress, Charlie thought, for the amount of effort that had gone into it.

Charlie slipped his finger through the slot, being careful not to cut himself on a sharp edge, and got a better feel for what they were up against. It was one thing to think about three-quarter-inch thick steel in the abstract; it was quite another to span that much metal with your finger and think of boring through it with a hand drill!

Nevertheless, now that he'd begun to move about again, Charlie felt pretty good. Picking up the hacksaw that was lying nearby, he set to work, convinced that, as strong as he felt, he should be able to do great things. Disillusionment came swiftly. After five minutes Charlie's strength had vanished and his arms ached abominably. He sat back on his heels, gasping for breath, and looked at what he'd accomplished: barely enough to notice! Thoroughly chastened, he surrendered his place and descended into the motor room. After searching for a few minutes, he found a vacant spot beside a box of spare parts, slumped wearily against it, and fell asleep.

It was nearly midnight when Fred Whitehead reported back to the tiller room. Although the slot was now long enough to accommodate the hacksaw, it wasn't yet wide enough to allow the blade to turn sideways. According to the captain, that was their next goal. Refusing to be discouraged by their modest progress so far, Whitehead took over the ratchet drill and pitched in.

Presently the drill began to stick, as the teeth on the beveled gears became burred. Fred carried it down into the motor room to file them smooth, but when he brought the drill back, he was too tired to lift himself up through the doorway. Savvy sent him down to rest. Fred found a place at the forward end of the motor room, laid back against the same box of electrical parts that supported Charlie Grisham, and soon fell asleep too.

Not far from them, Henry Love lay propped against one of the air compressors. Henry had borne the brunt of much of the afternoon's events and was still trying to recover. After his struggle to halt the flooding in the torpedo room, he'd collapsed in one of the bunks in the battery room; but just as he'd started to feel better, the *S-Five* had tilted up and pitched him against the forward bulkhead. A moment later hundreds of gallons of water had come thundering into the compartment, bashing him against various hard, immovable objects. By the time he was rescued by Longstaff's curtain rope, Henry had swallowed even more water, not to mention fuel oil, and had inhaled a quantity of chlorine gas. Feeling thoroughly used up, he'd climbed into the conning tower with George Bill and the other sailors.

That had been a good decision. The close-packed bodies on the steering platform had kept Henry warm. By the time everyone was ordered to abandon the control room, he'd felt strong enough to climb up to the engine room under his own power. Apparently he hadn't recovered as much as he'd thought, because the climb had hit him hard. For a while he'd fallen asleep draped across the port diesel, until he'd been awakened by the sound of an explosion. The engine block had cooled by then and the air was getting thick, so he'd climbed up here into the motor room.

Henry looked around the darkened compartment and was

struck by its otherworldliness and silence. Other than whispers from some of the men who were still awake, the only sounds were the faint chink of tools from the tiller room and occasional deep groans from the hull. The regular lighting system had long since gone out, extinguished by the efforts to keep the electric drill going. Even the emergency lighting had faded. Henry had overheard Chief Otto muttering about low battery voltage. The result was a strange twilight that mutated shapes and made distances hard to judge. To compensate the electricians had set up extra lamps for the workmen, but these burned dimly too. Spilling out through the tiller room doorway, their sulfurous glow silhouetted the workers and sent goblin shadows leaping and jerking across the motor room walls.

### 23:50—Tiller Room.

Shortly before midnight Savvy was confronted by another problem. Careful rationing of the water that Grisham had brought from the control room had maintained the crew's fluid intake for an additional two hours, but now that supply was gone and thirst was sinking its implacable claws into everyone. Lack of water wasn't as dramatic as lack of air, Savvy reflected, but given enough time it would kill them just as surely. Like so many things that they couldn't control, it would also prevent them from working effectively. Now that so many men were packed into the stern, the air temperature had begun to rise, which would only add to the crew's discomfort and increase the rate at which they became dehydrated. Savvy searched his memory, trying to recall any other source of potable water in the sub. When he'd almost given up, he remembered the boat's emergency rations.

As unlikely as shipwreck might seem in 1920, every Navy ship carried a supply of preserved food in case the crew became stranded someplace. These stores didn't contain drinking water, but the liquid from the canned fruit and vegetables might keep everyone going a little longer. Unfortunately the "E-rations" were packed into a spare lubricating oil tank in the control room, and by now the air in that compartment was thoroughly tainted by chlorine gas. Dangerous as it would be to reenter the compartment, it was their only source of water. Climbing down into the motor room, Savvy asked if anyone would volunteer.

"I'll go!" Predictably it was Percy Fox. A few minutes later the Chief and two other sailors lowered themselves into the engine room and quickly pulled the watertight door closed. The pain from the chlorine was excruciating. Gagging and wheezing, they scrambled down to the storage tank and began fumbling at the hexagonal nuts that held the cover in place. It was impossible to remain at the tank for more than a few seconds at a time and they were already so weak that each of them could only loosen a few of the nuts, but somehow they got the cover off. Loading their arms with cans, they hurried back to the door, passed the cans through, and returned for a second load.

By their third trip to the storage tank, they had grown too weak to carry anything. Abandoning the cans they'd been trying to carry, they headed for safety. Luckily all of them made it under their own power, because if one had fallen, it's unlikely that the others could have carried him. Willing hands pulled them up through the doorway into the engine room, where they lay gasping and retching for some time before they could stand. In all they had retrieved more than two dozen large tins of fruit, beans and corned beef. The corned beef didn't have many takers, but the other cans provided refreshment and a welcome reprieve for many of the crew.

## THURSDAY, 02:00—MOTOR ROOM.

There was a muted thud and a deep tremor ran through the sub. The jolt woke John Longstaff, who was still sleeping on the engine room's forward bulkhead. He sat up quickly, trying to attach some significance to the half-remembered sound. The likeliest source, he decided, was an explosion in the battery room. With that thought he got hurriedly to his feet, but then he realized that, if it had been an explosion, there was nothing he could do about it. He hoped that the hull hadn't been weakened too much.

According to Longstaff's wristwatch, it was a few minutes after 2:00 A.M. He felt good compared to how miserable he'd been when they'd abandoned the control room a few hours earlier. Yawning and stretching, but fully awake at last, he started to climb, up over the rocker arms and then more slowly through the motor room. When he reached the top and looked back the way he'd come, he saw a remarkable tableau. Extending almost ninety feet straight down to the engine room bulkhead, the sub's darkened central passageway was lined by the hunched and twisted shapes of sailors clinging to machinery or propped up wherever they could find room. It was a dismal, almost infernal scene. In the darkness above him, he could see little except the glowing tiller room doorway and Chief Bender, patiently standing watch in the shadows beneath it.

Longstaff wanted to stay where he was, in the hope of being useful, but he couldn't locate a stable place to stand. Everything he might have used for support was too slippery with oil, so he climbed down to the crew's head several yards below the tiller room bulkhead. When he reached it, he discovered that it already held three men, leaving no room for him. Undaunted he gingerly tested the cubicle's door and, finding it strong enough to support him, stretched out to wait. After what seemed like ages, two sailors emerged from the tiller room, crept past Longstaff's refuge and disappeared into the murk of the motor room. As he clambered up to replace them, Longstaff concluded that the captain's plan for organizing the drillers had already broken down; the teams were no longer sticking together.

Pulling himself up through the doorway, Longstaff found the captain working on the hole, no surprise there. An Old Man had been set up and Savvy was using it with a ratchet drill. When he moved aside and Longstaff caught his first glimpse of the "escape hole," the *S-Five*'s junior officer froze, staring in consternation. After more than five hours of labor, it was merely a slot, about an inch wide and four inches long! At this rate it would take days to create an opening that a man could crawl through, even assuming they could continue working at the same pace. The thought spurred Longstaff to pick up the ratchet and attack the hole ferociously. For about ten minutes he pushed and pulled with all his strength, but, as far as he could tell, it made little difference. In a very short time he could barely pull the ratchet over and he had to relinquish his spot.

Before leaving, Longstaff pulled himself close to the hole and, under the pretext of looking out, leaned close enough to draw a breath of fresh air. It was like a taste of heaven! Only the greatest exercise of will power enabled him to pull away from and crawl back out of the tiller room.

### 05:30—Tiller Room.

At dawn Chief Whitehead climbed back into the tiller room. Several hours of sleep had revived him considerably in spite of his cramped position against the packing crate, and he went back to work with renewed determination. Before beginning to drill, he peered through the hole at the glimmer of first light on the water, and heaved a deep sigh. Stretching away to a barely perceptible horizon, the Atlantic Ocean had never looked so enticing. Picking up a hammer and chisel, Whitehead began chipping at the hole's ragged margin.

The hole itself had been transformed by daylight. No longer a somber black bar, it glowed with a pearly radiance that spread through the tiller room and sent pale reflections beyond the doorway into the motor room. The sight of daylight painting gossamer patterns on the steel walls seemed to raise everyone's spirits.

When the sun cleared the horizon a short time later, the world beyond the hole expanded into a vast blue-green wedge and Savvy began halting work every five minutes to look outside. His vantage point appeared to be about ten feet above the surface, which reassured him about the danger of swamping. From the angle of the sun, it appeared that he was looking due south. By pressing his face close to the hull and shifting from side to side he could see about a third of the horizon. The rest was a mystery.

Because the sub's bow rested on the bottom, the hull didn't move much in the swells. During darkness this had worked to their advantage, since hour after hour of erratic bobbing would have troubled even the most hardened sailor's stomach. Now that daylight had come, however, Savvy began to regard this as a mixed blessing. In fact, he would have gladly traded comfort for a freely floating submarine, which would have gradually turned around and enabled him to see in every direction. For all he knew an entire squadron of ships might be anchored directly behind the *S-Five*, although he suspected that the ocean in that direction was just as barren as the part he could see. Nevertheless, help might appear at any time and from any direction, and he would have preferred to be able to see it coming.

Shortly after dawn a ship appeared. Savvy spotted it during one of his observation breaks and this first glimpse of a human presence on the empty sea was so unexpected and thrilling, that he thoughtlessly blurted it out to the men around him. Word spread rapidly through the sub, accompanied by a wave of excited murmuring, as crewmen shook their neighbors awake to tell them the good news. It gave Savvy a sense of the crew's desperation to see how quickly they jumped to conclusions.

"We're saved, boys!"

"There's a ship standing by!"

"It's only a matter of time now!"

The jubilant pronouncements brought smiles to the ravaged faces around him, but Savvy soon wished he hadn't spoken so precipitously. The ship was nearly ten miles off. At that distance the stern of the *S-Five* would be little more than an indistinct blot on the water, easy to overlook; and anyone who did notice it could easily disregard it as a bit of flotsam drifting around in the ocean. The sub's tail certainly wouldn't resemble any vessel.

Sure enough the distant ship continued without changing course and soon dropped out of sight. Savvy waited to be sure that it wasn't going to reappear before announcing the fact to the crew.

When he did, they responded with various emotions. Many were despondent, but a surprising number reacted angrily, swearing and banging their fists against bulkheads and lockers, outraged that a ship would pass a wreck at sea and not give assistance. Their vehemence convinced Savvy that he mustn't reveal anything that happened outside the sub, until he had a better idea of its significance. And so, when a second ship came into view an hour later, he quietly watched it sail out of sight without mentioning it to anyone.

By mid-morning their time appeared to be running out. For what it was worth, the chlorine gas was still confined to the forward compartments, but every man was panting now due to the rising level of carbon dioxide; and the steady decline in oxygen level weighted them all with such a deadening fatigue that only the most determined were able to move. These brave souls hauled themselves up to the tiller room, but often found that they couldn't lift the tools when they got there, and their movements were so lethargic that much of their time was spent merely getting into position. The organization into drilling teams had utterly disintegrated; anyone who had enough stamina to work was allowed to fill a vacancy as long as he could. The bad air was warm and therefore tended to collect in the upper parts of the sub, making it even harder for the men in the tiller room to accomplish anything.

Some of the men were coping better than others, but all had been pushed close to their limits. Sooner or later, Savvy knew, one of them was going to stop breathing. It would be a sign that the end was near for all. To stave off that moment, Savvy stationed one of his chief petty officers at the engine room's emergency oxygen cylinder—the last of their reserves, with orders to release small amounts at regular intervals; but the extra oxygen had no appreciable effect. Indeed, a short time later Savvy had to assign someone else to tend the cylinder, because the first man had lost consciousness! By noon the oxygen in the reserve tank had been exhausted, along with the last cubic foot of air in the air banks.

As if to leave no doubt of their fate, the S-*Five*'s stern appeared to be settling lower in the water. When Savvy called to check, the men in the engine room confirmed that the depth gauge needle was rising again. Savvy could only nod grimly. By allowing the air pressure inside the sub to decrease, their "escape" hole had made it possible for the sea to leak in even faster. Without an effective pump or compressed air, they could do nothing to stop it. The sub would continue settling lower and lower, until the bottom edge of the escape hole—presently about seven feet above the water— dropped even with the surface. From that moment their lives would be measurable in minutes.

At first seawater would flow into the tiller room. They'd abandon the compartment, of course, retreating behind the watertight door into the motor room, but that wouldn't stop the flooding. When the weight of water in the stern overcame the sub's remaining buoyancy, it would pull the *S-Five* back down to the bottom. This time, however, the tiller room would be open to the sea. Although the hull was designed to withstand 150 pounds per square inch, corresponding to a depth of about 300 feet, the internal bulkheads weren't as sturdy. At some point the motor room bulkhead would collapse, followed quickly by the engine room bulkhead. Assuming that the lights stayed on, oblivion would come in an instant of onrushing blackness and a soundless thunderclap. Looking at the slumped figures around him, Savvy wondered if that might not be the most merciful way for them to go.

Noon came, then 1:00. Virtually all the crew were incapacitated by now. What little energy they retained was consumed by the overwhelming labor of breathing. The sub's interior resounded with the stertorous rasp of men striving to get enough air into their lungs. For some the hardest effort they had ever put forth seemed like child's play compared to the labor of breathing. Writhing around in a corner of the tiller room, John Longstaff tried vainly to escape from the ache that enveloped his body, but no position afforded relief. Fred Whitehead lay in a heap beside the packing crate in the motor room.

Many more would have curled up and abandoned hope, if it hadn't been for the captain. In spite of the overwhelming odds against them, Savvy Cooke refused to admit defeat. He continued to chip away at the hole in the tiller room, ignoring the fact that he was making negligible progress. Every few minutes he put down his tools and scanned the horizon, which had remained empty since morning, trying not to think about the number of ships that might have passed outside his range of vision. As the afternoon progressed, he watched the sun slide down the sky with morbid fascination, knowing that the next time it passed this way, he and all his shipmates would be dead. With a sigh, he picked up the hammer and chisel and began tapping at the edge of the hole.

# 10

## THE *ALANTHUS*

"No man can be sure of his courage until the day of his death."

— Jean Anouilh

THURSDAY, SEPTEMBER 2, 14:00.

Twenty-four hours after the sinking, the interior of the *S-Five* resembled a tomb. Most of the crew had lost consciousness or lapsed into a state of apathy so profound that only the feverish rise and fall of their chests showed they were alive. A few retained enough strength and will to drag themselves up to the tiller room, but none of them had any hope of cutting a usable escape route. Sixteen hours of drilling, chipping, and sawing had produced a roughly triangular opening six inches wide and eight inches high. With the proper tools and able bodies, they might have created an escape hole in another twenty hours but that was twenty hours they didn't have. The only consolation for any of them was that the escape hole had been their best chance—their *only* chance—and they had given it their best shot.

As far as Savvy knew, none of the crew had died yet, but it could only be a matter of time. The thought of these brave men being snuffed out one by one was almost insupportable. Perhaps that's why he continued working on the hole so single-mindedly; the labor helped to distract him from what was to come. Each time he looked outside, the clouds were a little different and the sun had taken another small step across the sky, but otherwise nothing had changed on that great empty wilderness of water. There had been no ship since the two that had passed by early in the morning. In fact, Savvy had come to anticipate the same monotonous view so much that he almost overlooked the third ship.

Startled, he rubbed his eyes and peered again into the glare. No mistake: it *was* a ship! bearing almost due south and not more than five miles distant. But it was heading *away* from them. There was no time to lose.

"A ship! There's a ship!"

Weak as it was, his shout had a remarkable effect. Crewmen who moments before had seemed more dead than alive became revitalized.

"Where away?"

"What's she look like?"

"Has she seen us?"

Savvy ignored the questions. They had to make a signal: he bellowed, "Find matches! Paper! Anything that will burn!"

Men emptied their pockets, rooted through lockers, searched and searched again, but all in vain. The repeated flooding had soaked everything in the sub so thoroughly that there wasn't a dry match to be had, nor any dry paper to burn, if they'd found a match. Savvy kept an eye on the ship during the search. The possibility that it might pass out of sight without stopping was ghastly, but he knew how easily that could happen. If the ship had posted a lookout—although many did *not*—any one of a multitude of minor distractions might allow the *S-Five* to slip by unnoticed. Even if someone spotted the sub, there was no compelling reason to investigate her. She could be a bit of wreckage, a stray buoy . . . almost anything. In addition to attracting attention, Savvy and his shipmates had to demonstrate that this strange object contained men who needed help.

But how? Seconds flickered by, then minutes. The sense of frustration was an almost physical presence among them. The flooding and repeated upheavals had turned the interior into a waterlogged ruin and destroyed the materials that Savvy and his men might have used to make a signal. Savvy looked through the hole again. The ship hadn't changed its heading. In ten, maybe fifteen minutes it would pass out of sight.

What about a spark from the electrical system? someone suggested.

Crewmen began sorting through the rags that littered the motor room, searching for the driest and oiliest scraps, while Nelson and Otto cobbled together a crude spark generator from the emergency lighting system. By now they'd become oblivious to electrical shocks, having endured so many of them from the drill; but, no matter how carefully they positioned the scraps of fabric between the electrodes with their scorched fingers, they couldn't get anything to burn, couldn't elicit so much as a wisp of smoke. By now Savvy was craning his neck to keep the vessel in sight. And then . . .

Savvy never learned who found the copper pipe, but the moment it appeared, everyone recognized its potential. Ten feet long, half an inch in diameter, it would make a perfect flagpole. All they needed was a flag.

Something white, Savvy admonished, so it would be easy to see.

But it wasn't easy to find anything white. The ubiquitous diesel oil seemed to have dyed every shred of fabric in the sub a dark shade of brown. At last a young second-class seaman dug deep into the bottom of his duffel bag and brought out a clean white T-shirt. Binding it to the end of the pipe with wire, they thrust the makeshift flag out through the hole and began waggling it furiously back and forth, using the edge of the hole as a fulcrum. Every minute or two they stopped, so that Savvy could peek out at the ship.

Waving the flag was hard work. Even when men paired up and pulled the end back and forth between them, it was exhausting; but there was no shortage of volunteers. News of a ship had galvanized everyone. Men thronged into the space below the tiller room door, peppering those above them with queries and relaying information to their shipmates further down in the sub. But for a long time there was nothing new to tell. The ship continued south, drawing steadily nearer to the point where it would drop below the horizon. As if the men sensed this, the questions became more pointed, the comments edged with desperation.

Just when it seemed hope was lost, the ship came about.

## TUESDAY, AUGUST 31, 1920, 15:15— NEW YORK HARBOR.

On a fair Tuesday afternoon the S.S. *Alanthus* sailed out of New York Harbor on what was to be her last voyage. Owned and operated by the Potter Transportation Company of New York, the little wooden steamship had outlived her usefulness and was being sent to the James River Shipyard in Newport News, Virginia to be "laid up." This was the nautical equivalent of being put out to pasture, except not so nice. She'd be tied to a broken-down dock someplace, and, if she was lucky, she might someday serve as a storage barge. More likely, however, she'd be auctioned off to the "knacker's yard" to be broken down for scrap or perhaps merely left to rot in some stagnant creek. It was a shame. The *Alanthus* was only two years old. Beneath a layer of grime she was a handy little vessel, with a high bow and single black smokestack rising through the two-story superstructure behind her bridge; but at slightly over 2,500 tons she was simply too small. She'd been built in Kearny, New Jersey during the war years, when ships of all types and sizes were at a premium. A little "coaster" like the *Alanthus* could make a decent living then; but, now that the war was over, a horde of larger merchant ships, newly released from military service, was competing for the civilian trade, and the *Alanthus* couldn't pay her way.

In command was Captain Earnest A. Johnson, sometimes known as "Twenty-One Knot" Johnson. A stout, barrel-chested man with a broad red face and big square hands, Johnson was born in 1884 on Saba, a small, mountainous island in the Dutch West Indies. He'd left home at the age of sixteen to go to sea. During the next twenty years he'd worked his way up from common sailor to licensed master, serving in practically every type of vessel afloat, from small schooners to big square-riggers and from harbor tugs to thousand-ton steamers. Along the way he'd survived earthquake, volcanic eruption, and convoy duty in the North Atlantic. He'd even panned for gold in the American West. Between voyages Captain Johnson made his home in the town of Richmond Hill, New York, where he lived with his wife and daughter.

Johnson had commanded the *Alanthus* since August 1, 1919, an eventful year that had taken the ship from New York to the Caribbean, through the Panama Canal, and down the west coast of South America. Like many hard-working ships, the *Alanthus* had been plagued by breakdowns, which hadn't been helped on this last voyage by an incompetent and dishonest crew. By the time the ship docked in the small port of Tocapilla in Chile, Captain Johnson was gravely ill with yellow fever. At first he resolved to lay over in Tocapilla until he had recovered, but in January he discovered that members of the crew were plotting to turn the ship over to local pirates. Jaundiced and with a raging fever, Johnson took the *Alanthus* to sea. After two horrific days steaming north along the coast, a crewman sabotaged the steering gear, hoping to force the ship into the port of Callao in Peru. By steering his ship from the tiller room for two more days with a pistol strapped to his hip, Johnson managed to reach Balboa, Panama, where he was taken ashore by the local authorities more dead than alive. Against all odds he survived, and in February, with a new crew, he arrived safely back in New Orleans. For the next eight months the *Alanthus* sailed in the coastal trade along the Gulf of Mexico, until her owners decided that it had become too expensive to maintain such a small ship and called her back to New York.

Merely getting away on the present voyage had been a struggle. The glut of postwar shipping had made it difficult to obtain cargos, and an oversupply of qualified seamen had resulted in wage reductions and retaliatory strikes by the sailors. For days the little steamship had remained in New York Harbor, tied to the pier while moorage fees piled up and Captain Johnson tried to find a paying consignment for the trip to Virginia. Perversely, just when he succeeded in arranging for a small shipment of coal, his deck crew walked off the boat, vowing not to sail for the low wages they'd been promised. Hurrying out into the labyrinth of bars, pawnshops, and cheap hotels that bordered the wharves, Johnson put together a skeleton crew and set sail immediately, before any other disaster could intervene.

As a result, the *Alanthus* sailed without her radio operator, who had gone ashore for some last-minute shopping half an hour before Johnson's abrupt decision to sail. The ship's third officer had known about the errand, but in the hurry of departure, he hadn't thought to check the crew manifest to see if everyone was back aboard. By the time he remembered, the *Alanthus* had rounded Boston Light and was heading out to sea. They could have gone back, but Captain Johnson had sailed most of his life without benefit of a radio and he wasn't about to turn around now for lack of one.

### THURSDAY, SEPTEMBER 2, 13:15— OFF NEW JERSEY.

By Thursday afternoon the *Alanthus* had reached Latitude 38.49 N and Longitude 73.51 W, putting her about fifty miles southeast of the Delaware Capes. The day was cool and sunny, with a moderate sea running, and the little ship was steering a course of 220 degrees, almost directly into the afternoon sun. Chief Engineer Carl Jakobsen and Assistant Engineer "J. J." Hurt were walking along the deck, talking and looking out over the sea. As they paused at the starboard rail amidships, Hurt shaded his eyes and peered more intently toward the north. "What do you make of that?" he asked, pointing to a small dark object silhouetted on the horizon. At first Jakobsen thought it might be the tail of a downed airplane, but neither he nor Hurt could be certain. In fact, after scrutinizing the strange outline through their binoculars, they could only agree that it didn't resemble anything they'd ever seen before. To be on the safe side, they decided to report what they'd found to Captain Johnson on the bridge.

Johnson examined their discovery through his own binoculars for several minutes before announcing that it was nothing more than a fishing boat. Unconvinced, Jakobsen and Hurt resumed their stroll on the deck, but they continued to watch the mysterious shape as the *Alanthus* drew away toward the southeast. It had nearly fallen out of sight altogether, when Jakobsen noticed a small white "rag," as he called it, fluttering back and forth along one side. The rag moved jerkily, starting and stopping at irregular intervals. They were sure it hadn't been there before. Even if this was a fishing boat, something was very wrong! The engineers hustled back to the bridge to inform Captain Johnson. A few minutes later the *Alanthus* turned hard starboard and headed north.

**14:15—The *S-Five*.**

*Binoculars!* Savvy thought regretfully, as he squinted into the afternoon sun. He should have told Grisham to salvage a pair of binoculars before abandoning the control room, but it was too late to correct the oversight. Without the glasses he had to wait until the ship was less than a mile away to form a clear impression of her: a small steamer, two or three thousand tons displacement, the kind of coastal trader that had been common around the turn of the century. After her initial course change, she gave no further indication of having seen the *S-Five*. Savvy encouraged the flag wavers to maintain their efforts. Nothing would be worse than seeing their potential rescuer abandon them, when her curiosity had been satisfied. Minutes later, with the awful perversity that had hounded the *S-Five* since the crash dive, that's exactly what happened. At a distance of several hundred yards, the little ship turned and, as Savvy watched in stunned silence, began steaming eastward. Within minutes she had passed out of his range of vision.

In desperation Savvy began shoving trash out through the hole, calling to the men below to shred any paper they could find into streamers that might be taken up by the wind. Jamming himself as far back into the stern as possible, he stuck his arm out through the hole and waved frantically. He even went so far as to put his face up to the hole and shout as loudly as he could. When he paused to catch his breath, the men waving the flag redoubled their efforts, grunting and gasping, as they hauled back and forth on the pipe and jerked it violently in and out. Five minutes passed, then ten, and still no ship appeared. Finally Savvy told the flag-men to cease. There was no sense in squandering their remaining strength in futile signaling. Instead he set them to work drilling new holes while they were still vitalized. As their excitement and hope faded, so too would their ability to push themselves beyond their limits.

In Savvy's opinion the disappearance of third ship was the most terrible moment the crew suffered. To have the ship turn and leave them to their fate, just as they were congratulating them-selves on their impending rescue, was almost more than they could bear. Some of them were apathetic. Others—a surprising number—were angry.

"Where the hell's he goin'?"

"Can't the bastard see?"

"Damn his eyes anyway!"

But nothing they said could alter what had happened. It was the final blow to all their hopes.


**14:30—The *Alanthus*.**

As the *Alanthus* bore down on the apparition, off-duty crewmen lined the rail, inspecting it with a rag-tag assortment of binoculars and pocket telescopes, and, in the manner of sailors everywhere, laying bets: it was the tail of an airplane, the crow's nest of a sunken ship, a derelict oil tank . . . Soon all of them could distin-guish Jacobsen's white "rag" snapping back and forth beside the object, but they still couldn't make out a human form or any other recognizable activity. Was the rag merely a bit of debris flapping in the breeze, or a bird caught in some rigging? Finally, when the distance had narrowed to only a couple of miles, it became evident that the object was the stern of a large submarine rising at a steep angle out of the sea. The bettors all took back their wagers. No one had guessed correctly.

When the *Alanthus* was within several hundred yards of the stricken submarine, Captain Johnson changed course and circled around behind, in order to examine it from every angle. When he was sure that the *S-Five* posed no hidden threat to his ship, he hove to and lowered a boat. Leaving his first mate in charge of the *Alanthus*, he ordered the boat crew to row to within twenty yards and again circle the sub. From this distance he could make out details: the two-foot brass propellers with their trailing rudders, the twin diving planes, and high on the sub's starboard side a small ragged hole. The flag—Johnson had long since identified it as a man's undershirt fastened to a length of pipe—no longer extended from the hole and the bits of trash and ragged streamers of paper that had emerged to flutter away in the breeze had stopped as well. Nevertheless, Johnson and his men had no misgivings. This was not a derelict; there were people inside. Captain Johnson had his rowers pull the boat up under the hole so that he could hail them.

"What ship are you?" he bellowed.

## 14:45—The *S-Five*.

Twenty minutes after it had vanished, the little white steamship sailed back into view. This time it was much closer. Its reappearance had an electrifying effect on the crew. No one doubted now that they'd been found. The buzz of elated talk resumed, as the men in the tiller room tried to keep the rest informed about what was happening.

"Where is she now?"

"Coming right toward us."

"She can't be making much speed."

"That's okay. I think she sees us all right."

"It's taking her a hell of a while to get here!"

The ship vanished again, but this time the men weren't disheartened. It made sense, they assured each other. No sensible skipper would risk his ship near a half-submerged wreck without first looking it over. In spite of their newfound confidence, however, all of them waited tensely for the ship to come back into view. At last there was a dull scrape and thump against the hull. The men who had gathered below the tiller room froze in anticipation. It was 2:45 in the afternoon.

From outside the sub a heavily accented voice hailed, "What ship are you?"

Savvy placed his mouth as near to the hole as he could and tried to keep his voice from cracking, for he was hoarse from shouting. "Submarine *S-Five*," he answered.

"What nationality?"

"United States."

"Where are you bound?"

At that Savvy's mordant sense of humor, never far below the surface, broke through. "To Hell!" he roared back. "By compass!" The men around him broke out in snickers and guffaws. After an uncertain pause Captain Johnson introduced himself and gave the name of his vessel. He desired to know how he might be of assistance. Savvy quickly outlined their plight and told Captain Johnson that the best thing he could do for them was to get them out of the sub quickly. To his dismay, it quickly became evident that this might not be possible at all. According to Captain Johnson, the *Alanthus* had virtually no tools for cutting through metal: no drills, no hacksaws, no cold chisels . . . nothing.

"Shall we take you in tow?" Johnson suggested, outlining a plan to tow the *S-Five* into the shallow water inside the Delaware Breakwater, where rescue efforts would be easier.

The thought of the little steamship attempting to pull his flooded submarine forty or fifty miles to the Delaware coast horrified Savvy. The first tug on the *S-Five*'s stern would almost certainly pull her under water, flooding the tiller room and quite possibly sending her to the bottom. In the unlikely event that the sub didn't sink and the *Alanthus* could pull her, there still wasn't enough breathable air. By the time they reached a port or the nearest shoal, Savvy and all his men would have perished.

"No!" Savvy replied quickly. "Do *not* attempt to tow us."

"Then how can we help you?" Johnson asked.

"We need air," Savvy told him. "Air and water! As soon as possible. And we need you to make us fast to your ship. We're sinking!"

### 15:10—The *Alanthus*.

His thoughts whirling, Earnest Johnson had his men row back to the *Alanthus*. Back on board his ship, he began dividing his men into work parties. Normally the little steamer carried a complement of fifty men, but on this voyage Johnson had been forced to sail shorthanded. If he kept a bare minimum on watch to run the ship, he could assign a dozen men to work with his engineers and the same number to help him secure the submarine.

Going astern at slow speed to align his ship with the *S-Five*, Johnson steered the *Alanthus* directly toward the submarine, with her engines on dead slow and her propellers barely turning over. When the little steamer's bow had nudged up against the sub's stern, he put his best steersman on the wheel with instructions to hold her steady in that position. Then he hurried down to the boat deck, where a picked crew was waiting.

For nearly an hour Johnson and his men struggled to drag a new five-inch Manila hawser around the *S-Five*, thread it between the propeller shafts, and pass it up to the steamer's forecastle. Manhandling the bulky hemp in the swells beneath the sub's sharp-edged propellers and heavy rudders was tricky and dangerous work, but they pushed ahead as rapidly as possible in order to take advantage of the good afternoon light. With the *S-Five* tethered to the *Alanthus* at last the deck gang made the hawser fast to the bow windlass and engaged the clutch. With much clanking and rattling the *S-Five* was brought slowly up against the steamship's side.

When the cable was as tight as Johnson dared make it, men clambered across onto the submarine's stern and passed chain slings around the propeller shafts and struts, securing these with three-inch steel cable. In the end the *S-Five* was bound as firmly to the side of the little steamship as they could manage. If she was going to bottom now, Johnson reflected, she'd have to take the *Alanthus* with her. This wasn't as unlikely as it might seem. At 267 feet and 2,500 tons, the steamship was shorter than the sub and barely three times as heavy. In tying the two vessels together Johnson and his crew were risking both their ship and their lives.

When all was secure, Johnson's deck crew used a ladder to bridge the gap between the *S-Five* and the *Alanthus's* railing. Then they passed heavy sixteen-foot planks across the submarine's propeller struts and lashed these together, creating a sturdy platform about six feet above the water and three feet below the hole in the sub's stern. After more than an hour of back-breaking labor, they were ready to meet the trapped submarines.

Captain Johnson was the first to approach the hole. Its serrated border revealed at once how it had been fashioned. Considering the conditions that must exist inside the sub, Johnson marveled at the discipline and determination required to make it. Moments later, in what must be one of naval history's most unusual encounters, the two commanding officers faced each other. In terse sentences Captain Cooke described the dire state of his crew. He concluded by reiterating his plea, "We need air and water as soon as possible!"

Now Captain Johnson and his engineers were in a quandary. The *Alanthus* carried neither cutting torch nor power tools, and her hand tools were, if anything, inferior to those on the sub. Thus, while they could supply water to the trapped submariners easily enough, providing breathable air and fashioning a way out of the sub would be difficult, if not impossible. Fortunately, like all good engineers, Carl Jakobsen and J. J. Hurt were expert improvisers. While some of the deckhands ran to fetch water, the engineers set about concocting a way to force air into the sub.

It would have been simple, if the *Alanthus* had a compressed air system like the submarine's, but it didn't. On the other hand, it *did* have an ice machine. While Jakobsen went to work with hammer and chisel rounding off the sharp edges around the escape hole, Hurt began putting together a makeshift air system. First he disassembled the ice machine to get at the air compressor in its refrigeration unit. Then he connected the compressor to the ship's fire system, replacing the original water injector. Finally he ran several lengths of two-inch hose from the forecastle fire hydrant out onto the wooden staging beside the sub. By this time Jakobsen had finished smoothing the hole. They began feeding the hose into the sub, continuing until the men inside told them it had reached the engine room bulkhead.

Shortly after 4:00 P.M., Jakobsen and Hurt were ready. They cranked up their jury-rigged system, and air began flowing from the compressor through the ship's fire system, out the forecastle hydrant and down the hose into the sub. Within minutes they could tell that it was working. "You could see, hear, and smell the foul air escaping from the hole!" Jakobsen recalled.

The air hose was certainly a psychological boost for the *S-Five*'s crew. When Johnson asked Captain Cooke about the air quality in the sub an hour later, the *S-Five*'s commanding officer replied that it had "improved considerably." However, as time passed, the air didn't seem to make much difference in the crew's physical condition. Except for the handful of men who could crowd around the end of the hose, most of the crew continued to deteriorate. Evidently the *Alanthus*'s little makeshift air compressor couldn't keep up with the respirations of forty men, although it might buy them additional time.

Water had a more immediate and gratifying effect. Using buckets and a funnel the men on the staging directed a stream of fresh water through the escape hole, where it was caught in cans and passed down through the sub. Parched though they were, the men in the tiller room passed those first cans along untouched, so that their shipmates farther along could drink first, but eventually everyone was satisfied. "That blessed cold water," as Fred White-head called it, gave them a new lease on life. How permanent it would be remained to be seen.

# 11

## THE *GOETHALS*

*"Possunt, quia posse videntur."*—They can, because they
think they can.

—Virgil

THURSDAY, SEPTEMBER 2, 16:00—
THE *ALANTHUS*.

With fresh water being funneled into the sub and the makeshift
air pump chugging away in the background, Captain Johnson and
his engineers turned to the primary problem of getting the
trapped men out of the submarine. Since the *Alanthus* had no
drills or cutting tools of her own, the sub's captain had suggested
that they use his tools. It was an obvious and sensible suggestion,
for the men in the tiller room had grown so weak by now that the
tools were of little use to them. Unfortunately, when the drills
were passed out through the hole, it became evident that they
might be of little use to *anyone*. Almost twenty hours of continu-
ous hard usage had taken a severe toll of them: the breast drill's
hand crank rattled loosely and the ratchet jammed and skipped.
Many of the bits were chipped and blunted. Jakobsen and Hurt
spent precious time refurbishing the drills and sharpening the bits
with a hand file. By the time they were ready to begin work on the
hole, the sun was paving a dazzling copper highway into the west.

Using a sharp scribe, the engineers outlined a rough oval on the submarine's hull. Including the triangular gap that had already been cut from the inside, this would produce an escape hole about fourteen inches wide and eighteen inches high. The next step was to center-punch drilling points around the oval, spacing them about half an inch apart. By the time they had finished, there were 102 drilling points around the oval. And the magnitude of the task they had set themselves was becoming apparent. They were tiring, but there was no time to rest. It was nearly five o'clock, when Jakobsen positioned the drill carefully against the hull, settled its blunt end against his shoulder and began slowly turning the hand crank. A thin steel sliver spiraled out from the drill point.

The men inside the submarine followed the progress of the drilling with rapt attention. Those who were near enough to see into the tiller room responded with faint cheers as each new drill hole appeared, and relayed jubilant reports of every advance to the men below them. Savvy shared their enthusiasm, but he was also concerned. The engineers on the *Alanthus* had some advantages over the men working from below. For instance, they could lean into the drill, as the men in the tiller room could not. Compared to the men inside the tiller room, the men outside were relatively fit and rested, and they were breathing clean air instead of the foul stuff inside the sub. Yet to Savvy's eyes the escape hole progressed with painful slowness. As he watched the drilling, Savvy ran through a quick mental calculation.

Jakobsen and Hurt were currently taking between ten and fifteen minutes to drill each hole. This was significantly faster than Savvy and his men had been able to achieve. Nevertheless, even ignoring the time required to cut away the metal tabs left by the drill, Savvy estimated that it would require the better part of a day to complete the escape hole. Could he and his men survive for another day? He didn't think so. He'd already concluded that the makeshift air pump on the *Alanthus* couldn't keep them going indefinitely.

The same thoughts had occurred to Captain Johnson. In his opinion the additional air was doing a better job of maintaining the trapped submariners' morale than it was of keeping them healthy. The last time he'd spoken to Captain Cooke, the man had been breathing so hard that he no longer spoke in complete sentences, but in short bursts between breaths. His pronunciation was slurred as well. In the dim light of the tiller room, the submarine commander's face had appeared pale and shrunken, his eyes puffy and bloodshot. Was this merely the result of fatigue? Or something more sinister?

Modern science tells us that, when the oxygen level in air falls below about three-quarters of its normal value, judgment and physical condition begin to fail. Captain Johnson obviously didn't think in these terms, but he suspected that Cooke and his men were showing signs of their ultimate decline, and he was sure that the time in which they could be saved was growing rapidly shorter.

Johnson had already posted a lookout at the *Alanthus's* masthead and ordered his bosun to prepare the international distress signal. Now he added the flags for "Come nearer at once." If a ship appeared, he intended to be ready.

But there had been no ships all afternoon. By the time the drilling started, the sun was dropping toward the horizon. Once darkness fell, it would be much more difficult to attract attention. The *Alanthus* had a few signal rockets in her emergency chest, but not many. For the hundredth time Captain Johnson regretted not going back for that radioman in New York. As daylight waned he prowled around his ship: across the ladder to the scaffolding, up to the bridge, then back again to watch the drilling. Jakobsen and Hurt were doing their best, pushing the drills—and themselves— as hard as they could, but progress was still agonizingly slow.

It was nearly 5:00 when the masthead lookout sang out, "Ship. Ship to starboard!" The *Alanthus's* captain hurried up to the bridge. Following the lookout's direction, he saw a stain of smoke on the starboard quarter far to the south. After twenty minutes of impatient watching the distant ship was hull up on the horizon. "Hoist away!" Johnson ordered. The signal flags fluttered aloft, and he trained his binoculars on the other vessel to see if she would respond.

## THURSDAY, 17:00—THE *GOETHALS*—
## OFF NEW JERSEY.

Built in Germany in 1911, the S.S. *General George W. Goethals* was a 4,800-ton passenger steamer owned by the Panama Railroad and Steamship Company of New York. Because so much of their business went through the Panama Canal, her American owners had named her for the famous Army engineer who had completed the canal's construction in 1914. After serving as a troop ship during World War I, the *Goethals* had resumed her regular civilian duty, carrying passengers and freight between the eastern United States and the Caribbean. On the evening of September 2, 1920, she was forty miles off the New Jersey coast, steaming north on her way back to New York from the island of Haiti. On the bridge was Captain E.O. Swinson, the *Goethals's* former first officer, now making his first voyage as the ship's commanding officer. Although he was in his late thirties, Swinson looked younger. Of medium height with a lean build, he had dark hair and pleasant features marked by high cheekbones and an engaging smile.

Command of the *Goethals* was an important milestone for Swinson and he was determined to make a good showing on his first trip. That included arriving in New York Harbor on time. Consequently, when the lookout first reported another ship in the distance, Swinson's main concern was to steer well clear of her; but when the lookout called again to report that the ship was flying distress flags, the *Goethals's* captain promptly forgot about the schedule. Enacted in response to the *Titanic* tragedy, maritime law required ships at sea to respond to all distress signals; but beyond that it was part of the unwritten code of the sea, a tradition based on the knowledge deep within every seaman from captain down to lowliest boiler-room stoker that the next distress call might come from his own ship.

Within minutes the *Goethals* was steaming north at full speed toward the other vessel, which was about seven miles distant. It soon proved to be a small steamer about half the *Goethals's* size.

By this time Swinson had identified her from the number included in her hoist; she was the *Alanthus,* a freighter out of New
York. From a distance she appeared to be moored beside a large,
strangely shaped buoy; but as the *Goethals* drew nearer, it became
evident that she was tied to the stern of a large submarine protruding from the sea.

Unwilling to risk his ship unnecessarily by steaming too close to
this bizarre arrangement, Captain Swinson had the *Goethals*
heave to several hundred yards away. It was 5:40. Even before the
larger ship had stopped moving, the *Alanthus* had lowered a boat,
which began pulling rapidly across the intervening water. Meanwhile the smaller ship's captain hailed Swinson by megaphone. By
the time the *Goethals* had set her anchor, Johnson had acquainted
Swinson with the pertinent facts about the *S-Five* and the plight of
her crew.

When the *Alanthus*'s boat pulled alongside, Captain Swinson
delegated several of his officers to return with it to the other ship.
To help with the drilling, he sent Chief Engineer William Grace
and First Assistant Engineer Richard McWilliams. Captain Johnson had revealed that the *Alanthus* had a radio, but no operator,
which explained why the little steamer had relied on signal flags
instead of wireless to send the distress call. Swinson dispatched
his chief radio operator, Charles Asche, who would use the radio
to call for additional help and send reports back to the *Goethals.*
Since the smaller freighter also lacked a physician, Swinson ordered his surgeon, Dr. James Solsberg, to go along, too.

As the four officers prepared to descend the ladder into the
waiting boat, one of the *Goethals*'s passengers hurried across the
deck. He was Dr. Alfred Champion, a Navy lieutenant from Le-
long, Texas, on his way back to the States from medical duty in
Haiti. When he learned about the trapped men on the submarine,
Dr. Champion rushed to his cabin to retrieve his medical bag and
now offered to go along as Dr. Solsberg's assistant. Captain Swinson agreed; if the submariners' condition was as poor as Johnson
had said, both physicians might be needed.

18:00—The *Alanthus.*

A few minutes after 6:00 the *Alanthus*'s boat pulled away from the *General Goethals* and started back across the darkening sea, while the remainder of the steamship's passengers and crew lined the rail to watch. By the time the boat had reached the *Alanthus,* the sun had nearly set. While the rowers steadied the boat against the steamship's side, the *Goethals*'s officers hurried up the ladder that had been put over the railing and reported to Captain Johnson.

A few minutes later Charlie Asche hurried across the narrow quarterdeck and climbed up to the tiny radio shack behind the bridge. It didn't take him long to discover that the *Alanthus*'s radio equipment wasn't as powerful as he'd hoped. In fact, under optimal conditions its range was probably less than twenty miles. To reach the mainland Asche would have to establish a radio link with the *Goethals* and relay messages through the larger ship's wireless. Luckily his assistant back on the *Goethals,* radio operator Harold Byers, was capable of handling that end. Once the two ships had exchanged call letters—LMTQ for the *Alanthus* and LHDT for the *Goethals*—they got to work.

Shortly before 7:00 on Thursday, September 2, 1920, the first news of the sinking of the *S-Five* reached the outside world via Cape May Naval Radio Station in New Jersey:

> From: S.S. Gen. Goethals. Lat 38.36 N, Long 74.00 W. Send destroyers with gear to relieve crew in submerged submarine, *S-Five.* Been in this condition thirty-five hours. Bring material for cutting through hull.

This was followed a few minutes later by a more elaborate message. Logged in at precisely 7:00, the second message read:

> Send all assistance possible. S.S. Alanthus holding S-Five head down. Crew under water thirty-six hours and

still alive. Send all assistance possible to save life and electric drills and other equipment to aid in cutting through side. Position is Lat. 38.36 N, Long 74.00 W.

At 7:05 the duty officer at the Cape May Radio Station placed an urgent telephone call to Rear Admiral Charles Hughes, the commandant of the Fourth Naval District in Philadelphia. Minutes later the *Alanthus*'s message was on its way by telegraph to the Bureau of Naval Operations in Washington, D.C. By 7:30 the secretary of the navy had been contacted at home and informed of the events taking place just offshore.

Did the name of the *S-Five*'s captain ring a bell in the secretary's memory? It should have, for this secretary was Josephus Daniels, the same man who had presided over the Navy Department during the Edison Battery debacle in 1915. In any event, telephone and telegraph lines were soon humming up and down the east coast, as orders flashed out to the commandants of the Third, Fourth, and Fifth Naval Districts, instructing them to report the status of any ships that could be dispatched to rescue the *S-Five*.

This wasn't a simple request. With the United States no longer at war, the Navy didn't routinely keep warships on alert and ready to sail in every port. Many of the vessels currently between missions were undergoing repairs and couldn't put to sea under any circumstance; and nearly all ships were short-staffed, their officers and crews ashore on liberty or leave.[10] In spite of these difficulties, within a few hours a number of commanders had recalled their crews or filled in their ranks with volunteers from other commands; but getting under way was not merely a matter of pulling away from the dock. In the days of coal-fired steam engines, it required a significant amount of time to fire up the boilers and build up sufficient steam pressure.

[10] Naval personnel went ashore in one of two ways: *Liberty* referred to short-term absences between normal duty hours, while *leave* involved formal relief from duty for more extended periods of vacation.

First to sail was the *Breckenridge*, a destroyer from the Fifth Naval District, which left Norfolk Harbor at 9:45 and headed down the Chesapeake Bay at flank speed. She was followed half an hour later by another destroyer, the *Preston*, which had stayed behind to load oxyacetylene torches, air hammers, and chisels. At 10:00 the commandant of the Fourth Naval District reported that the destroyer *Overton* had sailed from Philadelphia with "appliances on board for cutting hulls," while from the Third District came news that the destroyer *Bridgeport* had left New York Harbor at midnight.

Ships at sea had responded, too. Just outside New York Harbor the minesweeper *Brazos* learned of the sinking by wireless and abruptly headed back out to sea. Far to the south, where she was anchored in the Southern Drill Grounds off the Virginia coast, the battleship *Ohio* under the command of Captain John Halligan received an urgent "OpNav" dispatch at 10:00. Within an hour the big ship had aborted her training mission, off-loaded her civilian observers to a support vessel, and with her deck crew filling in to pass extra coal to the engine room, was steaming northward at maximum speed.

Throughout the remainder of the night and into Friday other ships left port, including the destroyers *Biddle, Putnam,* and *Quail* and the U.S.S. *Beaver,* a sub-tender stationed at the New London Submarine Base. The *Beaver* had just returned from convoying a division of submarines to Pearl Harbor. Her commanding officer, Captain Thomas C. Hart, was commandant of the Third Submarine Flotilla, the group to which the *S-Five* was attached. He was also Savvy Cooke's close friend. Hart first learned of the sinking at 10:30 on Thursday. Frantic to get under way, he was angered by "the mass of unimportant stuff on the air" that he felt had prevented his hearing about the accident sooner. He complained half-jokingly that a fellow captain, Lieutenant Commander Van de Carr, had "stolen" a destroyer—probably the *Preston*—in order to reach the accident sooner.

By midnight Thursday a total of nearly a dozen warships were heading toward the featureless point on their charts that marked the *S-Five*'s position. There was no need to urge them to greater speed; every man on those ships knew the odds against survival when a submarine went down. Within less than an hour, the *S-Five* had been transformed from a solitary, unknown shipwreck into the focus of a massive naval operation and the center of a communications network that covered the entire northeastern seaboard and extended far out to sea.

Coordinating this wireless web, Charles Asche on the *Alanthus* and Harold Byers on the *Goethals* remained at their telegraph keys all night, sending and receiving dispatches from the Navy, answering calls from merchant ships, and relaying messages between the two vessels. Only minutes after their initial distress call was sent, Byers passed on the welcome news that the Navy had responded:

Relayed from Govt to General Goethals—19:02: Two destroyers, Breckenridge leaving immediately from Norfolk followed by Preston in about an hour equipped with drilling devices. Destroyer Overton sailed from Philadelphia at 9:30 to your assistance also equipped for cutting through steel and with doctor aboard.—Chief of Naval Ops.

Captain Swinson added a question of his own for the *Alanthus:*

Is there any chance of our men cutting them out before the destroyers get here? If so we will stand by to receive them on board here.

The reply from the *Alanthus:*

Captain here says no assistance required except destroyers. Stand by until their arrival. Chance of cutting men out before midnight doubtful.

To which Swinson replied:

Will stand by as long as we are needed.

In addition to this type of exchange the two radio operators sent numerous "tactical" messages, as boats carrying men and supplies plied back and forth between the ships. From the *Goethals*, for example:

Is small boat alongside? Will come closer but don't want to run him down.

To this the *Alanthus* sent back a warning that the larger ship's wake might endanger the submarine:

Advise not to come too close [on] account of suction parting hawser.

During the night several merchant ships called to ask if they could be of assistance. Most, like the S. S. *Gulgoa* and the S. S. *Luckinbach,* were unable to offer anything more than additional manpower. Their offers were politely declined. Around midnight, however, the tanker S.S. *Hunt* sent this message:

We have apparatus for cutting: an electric drill. Will take about two hours to reach you. Do you want him?

This was good news. It had already become obvious that, in spite of the extra hands available, it would take many hours to open the *S-Five*'s hull; and no one was sure how much longer the trapped sailors would survive. Byers relayed Captain Johnson's response to the *Hunt*:

Please come with all speed!

When the tanker arrived several hours later, the *Alanthus* sent a boat to fetch the drill. Sadly it proved to be incompatible with the *Alanthus*'s electrical system. Simpson asked the *Hunt* to stand by, in any case, should extra help be needed.

IN THE *Alanthus*'s modest galley Dr. Solsberg and Dr. Champion began to organize their resources to care for forty sick and exhausted men, some of whom might be injured. After scouring the ship's stores for blankets and extra clothing, and sending a boat back to the *Goethals* for supplies, they instructed the *Alanthus*'s cook to start making soup, as well as pot after pot of hot black coffee (undoubtedly to restore the rescuers as much as the men they were working to save). Realizing that the *S-Five*'s crew would need sleep as much as anything else, the doctors commandeered all the available berths on the *Alanthus* and the mess hall too.

Engineers Grace and McWilliams took the ratchet drill they had brought from the *Goethals* and climbed over onto the scaffolding to relieve Jakobsen and Hurt. The *Goethals*'s engineers were a study in contrasts. William Grace was a handsome, vigorous man: big and broad shouldered, with thick wavy hair and deep-set, brooding eyes, an aquiline nose and broad sensuous lips. Robert McWilliams on the other hand was shorter, slender and dark, with straight black hair combed across his forehead and a quiet, almost diffident look. Dissimilar though they were, Grace and McWilliams had learned to work well together. After a brief assessment of what Jakobsen and Hurt had accomplished, they got down to business, allowing the *Alanthus*'s engineers to move on to another important project. With darkness falling fast, they needed to mount flood lamps on the *Alanthus*'s foredeck to illuminate the scaffolding.

With his powerful build and confident manner Bill Grace was the perfect sort of man to take charge in an emergency. Once a plan of action had been decided, he usually set to work as if he intended to complete the entire project single-handedly. In this case, that's exactly what he had in mind. Charlie Asche had sent word from the radio room that the Navy had acknowledged the distress calls and that ships were on the way, but there was no telling when they would arrive. From the way the men in the submarine were breathing, they must be in a bad way—and no wonder! Grace recoiled from his first look through the hole with an incredulous gasp. The air escaping from the sub was hot, malodorous, nauseating—and that was just the whiff he'd gotten out here on the scaffolding where it was diluted by cool, clean sea air. Grace could not imagine being immersed in air like that, yet these men had been obliged to breathe the awful stuff for more than a day. Grace had grave doubts that they would be able to survive much longer.

Weather was another factor. Grace cast a practiced eye at the sky. It was a cloudless night with a mild breeze out of the southeast and a calm sea heaving gently against the sub and her rescuer. The men in the *S-Five* had been extraordinarily lucky in having such fine weather, but it might not last. This was early September, the peak of the storm season. A gale, even a small one, would be disastrous, halting work on the escape hole, perhaps requiring the *Alanthus* to cast off from the sub to avoid being stove in. If that happened, the submarine would simply vanish, taking her crew with her.

As far as Bill Grace was concerned, the only way to avoid tragedy was to get those men out of the sub as soon as possible without relying on outside assistance. The thought must have crossed his mind momentarily that, if he'd had an acetylene torch, the task would require minutes instead of hours; but he didn't have a torch and one look at the strained, hopeful faces peering out of that hellish interior made him realize that he didn't care. He would get them out with the tools available. As Jakobsen and Hurt began stringing power cables across the *Alanthus*'s deck, Bill Grace stripped off his jacket, rolled up his sleeves and got to work.

19:00—The *S-Five*.

George Bill was crawling out of the tiller room when the engineers from the *Goethals* arrived on the staging outside. It was shortly after 7:00 P.M. and George was suffering so much from the bad air that he feared he might not live another hour. Then he heard the sound of a drill burrowing through steel and stopped to look up at the hull. There was something different about this sound, a sense of power and urgency that hadn't been there while the *Alanthus*'s engineers were at work. While he was watching, a new drill hole appeared. It seemed to take no time.

George felt a sudden, unexpected exhilaration. The men around him seemed to take heart too. Soon they were greeting each new drill hole with gruff applause, and passing word down to the rest of the crew. While some of the men were too incapacitated to speak, others responded excitedly:

"How many holes has he got now?"

"Sixty-seven, last count."

"Well, tell that guy to bear a hand!"

"Yeah, it's getting pretty tiresome down here."

Their new level of hope seemed to be fueled by the radiance spilling through the tiller room doorway. With the sub's exterior now brightly illuminated by search-lamps from the *Alanthus*, each new drill hole sent a brilliant shaft of light spearing down through the tiller room to ignite a glowing spot on its opposite wall. Hour after hour the work continued, with drill holes appearing at an amazing rate. Until now a single hole had required as much as a quarter of an hour; but the engineer from the *Goethals*, a big man named Grace, drove himself at such a furious pace that a new hole appeared every four or five minutes! Occasionally Grace was relieved by his assistant, a smaller man named McWilliams, who attacked the hull almost as fiercely, but mostly it was Grace, balancing on the narrow wooden trestle above the dark sea and working the ratchet with a ceaseless, pounding rhythm that echoed throughout the sub.

### 23:00—The *Alanthus*.

Grace and McWilliams worked tirelessly. By 11:00 the line of holes had arced around to form a semicircle; by midnight its ends had joined. All that remained was to cut out the remaining metal tabs between the drill holes with a hammer and chisel. Grace sent a sailor running up to the bridge to inform Captain Johnson that the end was in sight. Minutes later Charlie Asche tapped out a new message over the wireless:

> Expect to get men out shortly. Have you heard anything of destroyers coming to our aid?

The *Goethals* sent Captain Swinson's reply:

> Have heard nothing from destroyers yet.

But half an hour later at 12:35 A.M., the first of the Navy ships radioed the *Goethals*. From the destroyer *Brazos:*

> Proceeding your assistance. Arrive about four A.M. Please send your true position and what assistance I can render best.

Half an hour after that the *Billingsley* made a similar request.

Asche sent the messenger back to inform Grace and McWilliams that the nearest Navy ship was still two or three hours away; but the engineers no longer needed this intelligence. They were chipping away the last metal interstices that held the metal oval in place. They finished at 1:15 A.M.

Yelling to the men inside the sub to stand clear, Bill Grace rose up on the scaffolding with a ten-pound sledge in his hands. Balancing effortlessly above the water, his powerful shoulders glistening in the glare of the floodlights, the lines of his face cast in deep relief by a sheen of metal filings, he seemed more like the embodiment of some wrathful Norse god than the engineering officer of an American merchantman. Swinging the hammer high over his head, Grace paused for a moment in full extension, and then in a ripple of power, brought it down into the center of the oval. With one terrific blow he drove the metal plate crashing into the tiller room.

It was 1:20 A.M. on Friday, September 3, 1920.

Savvy Cooke had been awake continuously for nearly two days when the escape hole was finally completed. He'd spent the majority of that time in the tiller room either working on the escape hole himself or supervising the work of the others. By the time William Grace began chipping out the metal tabs around the circumference of their escape route, the *S-Five*'s captain was beyond mere exhaustion. For many hours he'd been on the verge of physical collapse, sustaining himself through sheer willpower.

John Longstaff and Percy Fox were with Savvy in the tiller room, when the hole was finally opened. In spite of their exhaustion, they watched with keen attention as the men on the scaffolding carved through the last metal strips that separated them from freedom. For Savvy it was a moment of profound emotion beyond personal happiness: for the first time since the *S-Five* had plowed into the sea floor, he could promise his men with complete sincerity that they would live.

There was a shout from outside, a moment of suspense, and then with a dull boom the metal plate jumped across the tiller room, bounced off the steering gears and clattered into a corner. After the hours of gloom inside the sub, the light that came flooding into the tiller room was blindingly bright and the gust of air that came with it was so pure and sweet that it made their heads swim.

Many of the sailors knew immediately that they'd been saved; others further down in the submarine didn't learn about it until more than an hour later, when the men above them began to climb toward the tiller room.

Moving all forty of the *S-Five*'s crew out through the escape hole proved to be more difficult and time-consuming than anyone had anticipated. Many of the submariners were so weak that they couldn't climb without assistance, and able-bodied shipmates had to stay below to help them. A seaman named Pendle—better known as "Hungry" Pendle—was the first man to emerge from the sub, followed by Percy Fox and John Longstaff. Although Longstaff had been with Savvy in the tiller room when the hole was opened, he didn't want to be the third man to leave the sub. By Navy tradition officers were the last to abandon ship, but with crewmen crowding up from below there was no place for Longstaff to move aside and Savvy reluctantly ordered him to climb out.

Getting up to the tiller room was the last hurdle for the *S-Fives*. Once they had reached the escape hole, strong hands were there to lift them out onto the scaffolding and assist them over to the *Alanthus*'s deck. This last step wasn't as difficult as it might have been, because Captain Johnson had foreseen that the trapped men would need help. While the final holes were being drilled in the sub's hull, he ordered several sailors to construct a double-legged canvas sling called a "bosun's chair." When the res- cued sailors had been secured in this, the ship's port side derrick hoisted them up and over the railing and deposited them gently on the steamer's deck. The chair was admirable foresight on Johnson's part, because none of the men from the sub could walk, much less negotiate the gap between the submarine and the *Alan- thus*. In spite of his fatigue, one young seaman insisted on trying to cross the steamer's deck under his own power but succeeded only in staggering in a zigzag pattern between the cargo hatch and the railing before two of the *Alanthus*'s crewmen caught him and helped him up to the galley.

As soon as they arrived there, the men from the *S-Five* were ex- amined by the surgeons in the small infirmary they had set up. If a sailor was pronounced fit, he was given coffee, hot soup, and warm clothing before being wrapped in blankets and packed off to one of the berths that had been set aside for them. Within minutes each was sound asleep. Four of the rescued men were deemed too sick to leave unattended. Three had developed respiratory prob- lems from the chlorine gas and the fourth, the sub's Filipino mess attendant, had several fractured ribs. These four were put to bed in the infirmary, where the doctors could watch them more closely.

While the first sailors from the *S-Five* were being cared for in the galley, out on the staging the evacuation continued at a steady pace. According to William Grace, many of the men who emerged from the hole had "a wild, haggard look with bloodshot eyes and swollen lips." It required three to four minutes to get each man out, but for the sailors still inside the sub it seemed to take much longer. George Bill remembers it this way: "The climb to the opening in the tail is hard to describe, but it was a tremendous climb for the condition we were in. You could feel your strength leaving the body and it seemed ages before we finally reached the top. The captain cheered us on as we reached the top."

Savvy needed to watch his men closely as they moved up toward the escape hole. Some had to be urged to move along faster; others had to be cautioned to take it easy, so that they wouldn't injure themselves in their haste. Just below the tiller room door, George Bill was about to take his turn in line, when he noticed that the gunner's mate next to him appeared to be fading fast. "Bear a hand here!" he yelled to the men above and began to assist the sailor upward. Several minutes later Bill discovered that the effort had cost him the last of his own strength. Just as he felt he couldn't hold on any longer, he felt a supporting hand. It was Lieutenant Grisham, who helped him up through the tiller room door. Here the captain greeted him with encouraging words and boosted him out through the hole, where the sailors from the *Alanthus* were waiting.

Charlie Grisham had been asleep on the motor room bulkhead when the escape hole was opened. He spent the next two hours helping the men around him start climbing. As he recalls, "This work seemed to have a bad effect on me and by the time I got up to the hole, I had decided that a man had to be pretty sick in order to die! My head ached so badly I could hardly see." When he had followed the last of the men up through the sub, he found Savvy Cooke alone in the tiller room.

"The captain had been sick for about twenty-four hours," Charlie recalled later, "And he looked pretty well used up."

Savvy climbed down to make sure that all of the crew had been evacuated from the sub. Then, while Grisham held a flashlight for him, he closed and carefully dogged the tiller room door to protect the *S-Five* from additional flooding. When he finally turned to follow his executive officer out through the escape hole, it was 3:34 A.M.

By this time Savvy was, to use Captain Johnson's laconic description, "in a bad condition." Nevertheless, when he reached the deck of the *Alanthus,* he insisted on verifying that all of his crew had received proper care. Only then would he allow himself to be examined by the doctors. When he was finally led up to Johnson's tiny cabin, he tumbled into the captain's bunk and fell instantly asleep.

THE MOMENT the hole into the tiller room was opened, Charlie Asche began sending the *Goethals* a running account of the rescue:

> Hole in submarine's side big enough to let men out. . . . First man removed one twenty a.m. . . . Twelve men removed. When all removed will decide transfer. . . . 40 men in crew. 26 out. . . . Only two men to come out. . . . All men on board S.S. Alanthus. Skipper off last. All men are in pretty bad shape but recovering now.

The *Goethals* in turn relayed the information to the Navy and to the S.S. *Hunt,* which in the best tradition of the sea had stood by faithfully until the last man was out. Before leaving, the tanker radioed back:

> As our assistance is not required, I will proceed. Best of luck to you all.

The last message that Charles Asche sent from the *Alanthus* read:

> Captain here says unnecessary to stay aboard longer. Inform
> Navy I am relieved by operator formerly on submarine.

With that Asche signed off and joined the rest of the men from the *Goethals*, climbing wearily over the side and into the waiting boats. As they rowed back to their ship, the moon was directly overhead, her gibbous orb flooding the sea around them with an opalescent glow. Two hours later, as the moon was sliding down the sky, the *Goethals* picked up her anchor and resumed her interrupted journey to New York. By dawn she was out of sight. Shortly after 6:00 that evening she arrived in Hoboken, New Jersey, where she was greeted by a small crowd of onlookers and a horde of newspapermen.

# 12

## AFTERMATH

*"En toute chose il faut considerer la fin."*—In all matters
one must consider the end.

— JEAN DE LA FONTAINE

FRIDAY, SEPTEMBER 3—OFF NEW JERSEY.

At 4:00 A.M. on Friday, the first of the Navy ships was sighted. This
was the destroyer *Breckenridge* out of Norfolk. Other ships arrived throughout the morning, until the *Alanthus* and the *S-Five*
were surrounded by a small flotilla of Navy vessels, including five
destroyers, the *Brazos,* and a Navy tug, the *Algorna,* that had
come out of New York. Dominating them all was the huge battleship U.S.S. *Ohio.* The last to arrive, she dropped anchor at 9:00,
long after the *Goethals* had departed.

Most of the *S-Five*'s crew slept late that morning. According to
the *Goethals*'s surgeon, Dr. Solsberg, they had been in remarkably
poor shape when they emerged from the sub. In fact, he declared,
as far as he was concerned, the rescue had been accomplished
"just in time." When Savvy woke just after dawn, he requested immediately to be put in contact with the senior officers on the Navy
ships. Now that Charles Asche had sailed away on the *Goethals,*
Frank Peters was the only radio operator on board the *Alanthus.*

Consequently, while his shipmates continued to sleep, poor Frank was awakened and pressed into service in the steamship's cramped radio room. There he stayed busy until midmorning "answering questions from every ship within range," in spite of the recurrent chills that wracked him, sometimes so severely that he "could not sit still for shaking." At 10:40 he sent:

> From U.S.S. Alanthus via Philadelphia to Operations Washington: U.S.S. S-5 secured to S.S. Alanthus about fifteen feet of stern above water—probably slight negative buoyancy—nose of boat on the bottom—vessels present U.S.S. Brazos, U.S.S. Overton . . . Alanthus proposed towing S-5 towards Delaware Capes. U.S.S. Brazos to take towing if Alanthus fails. Recommend service of Salvage Company be immediately obtained to render assistance off Delaware Capes.

By midmorning it was agreed that the *Alanthus* would make the first attempt to tow the *S-Five*. Ordering his crew to cast off the wire harness that had bound the submarine to his ship, Captain Johnson rang for "Dead Slow" on the engine room telegraph. The little steamer crept away from the *S-Five*, gradually taking up the slack in the towing cable that her crew had chained to the sub on Thursday evening. At a distance of about a hundred yards, the cable tightened and rose in the sea, bringing the *Alanthus* to a halt. Johnson rang for more steam. The propellers turned faster and the towing cable stretched tighter. The *S-Five's* stern tilted slightly in the direction of the tow, but neither sub nor ship moved. Johnson advanced the engine room telegraph step by step, until it stood at "Full Speed" and the little steamship's propellers were turning at a rate that should have produced better than ten knots. Her hull throbbed with the force of her engines, but the submarine stayed put, not even dipping below the surface.

It took only one trial to demonstrate the accuracy of Savvy's judgment: the *Alanthus* was too small to tow a water-logged sub as big as the *S-Five*. After less than an hour Johnson called it quits. At 10:40, after many heartfelt expressions of gratitude, the crew of the *S-Five* said goodbye to their benefactors and climbed over the side of the *Alanthus* for the short boat ride to the *Ohio*. The towing cable was brought over to the battleship too, and the *Alanthus*—free of her burden at last—departed for Norfolk. The story of the little steamship's role in the rescue had spread throughout the fleet and, as she sailed past the Navy ships their crews lined the rails to cheer her.

At 2:30 the next morning the *Alanthus* reached Sewell's Point on the southern lip of the Chesapeake Bay. Here Captain Johnson decided to lay over in order to give himself and his crew a well-deserved rest. By 3:30 that afternoon they were under way again for the short trip to Newport News. A few days later several miles up the James River in Virginia, the *Alanthus* dropped anchor and Captain Johnson walked off her bridge for the last time.

By 11:30 the *Alanthus* had disappeared over the horizon. The *Algorma* edged carefully alongside the *S-Five* and the tug's crew passed a two-inch steel hawser around the submarine's propeller struts, shackling it onto itself to form a crude harness. The arrangement proved to be inadequate; as soon as tension was applied to the cable, the sharp metal edges of the struts cut through it.

At 1:00 P.M. Captain Halligan ordered his engineers to replace the cable with something stronger. By evening the sub's stern had been wrapped in nine turns of inch-thick wire. For added security the *Alanthus*'s original hawser was left attached. With the *S-Five* now securely moored to the *Ohio*, officers from the various Navy ships gathered in the battleship's wardroom to decide the next step. In spite of the damage that the *S-Five* had suffered, the Navy wasn't about to abandon a brand new $1.5 million submarine without making an effort to recover her.

Before attempting to move the sub, Captain Halligan convened a formal board of investigation to collect evidence about the sinking. Savvy had asked Halligan to conduct the investigation promptly so that the *S-Five*'s crew could be sent home for some badly needed "rest and diversion." At 4:00 on Friday the panel of three senior officers met in the *Ohio*'s wardroom. Their first act was to have a boat lowered, so that they could examine the submarine themselves. Their findings confirmed what Savvy had already told them informally. Approximately fifteen feet of the sub's stern protruded from the sea at an angle of sixty degrees. The tiller room was flooded and bubbles of air were rising to the surface from the *inside*. Water was still leaking into the sub somewhere. Realizing that their window of opportunity for moving the *S-Five* would soon close, the Board returned to the *Ohio* and adjourned for the day. It was just after 5:00.

By this time the sub tender *Beaver* had arrived. As *S.O.P.*—Senior Officer Present—her commanding officer, Captain Hart, took charge of the proceedings. Hart initially favored pumping water out of the *S-Five*, starting at the tiller room and working toward the bow, while Captain Halligan, the *Ohio*'s skipper, favored towing the sub into shallow water before attempting to recover her. Once there, he argued, it would be less disastrous if she sank during salvage operations. Considering the late hour and the fact that the *S-Five* was already taking on water, Captain Hart changed his mind and endorsed Halligan's towing plan. After reaching the shallows, he reasoned, they could attempt to bring the sub to an even keel. If successful, they'd continue towing her to the Philadelphia Navy Yard; if not, they'd leave her on the bottom within the shelter of the Delaware Capes for the professional salvagers to raise. Because the *Ohio* was so much more powerful than the *Brazos*, it was decided that the battleship should make the attempt.

At 5:30, the *Ohio* moved slowly away from the *S-Five*, while deckhands on the battleship's fantail paid out the two-inch steel towing cable that they'd spent the afternoon attaching to the sub. At 100 yards they made the cable fast. As the *Ohio* continued to move, the submarine slid out of sight, drawn underwater by the combination of tension and the weight of the cable. Presently the *Ohio*'s stern dipped and her forward motion stopped.

Engine telegraphs rang for more steam and black coal smoke poured out of the battleship's funnels. At first nothing happened. The fact that the *Ohio* was pulling perpendicular to the plane in which the sub was tilted probably accounted for some of the resistance. The *Algorna* tried to nudge the big warship into the right orientation, but the strong set of the tide prevented her from completing the maneuver. There was no choice but to try to overpower the grip of the sea floor.

It took forty-five minutes for the battleship to break the sub free. As the *Ohio* moved forward at last and the towing cable slackened, Captain Hart speculated that the sub's port diving rudder, digging itself into the bottom like the fluke of an anchor, had been responsible for the resistance, and must have just broken off.

After the struggle to get started, the battleship made very slow progress. Coming slowly around to a course of 249 degrees, she steered toward Five Fathom Bank, fifteen miles from Cape May and the nearest shoal water. With her propellers turning for ten knots, the *Ohio* was making less than four knots; and the thick steel towing cable stretching back toward the invisible submarine was as rigid as a steel bar. It seemed evident that the *S-Five* was dragging along the bottom and digging in as she went. At this rate the *Ohio* would take all night to attain the off-shore shallows . . . if she could reach them at all.

After three miles of laborious progress, the procession was brought to a sudden halt. Evidently something big had snagged the *S-Five* or perhaps she'd fallen into one of the deep holes that soundings had indicated in the region. During the next half hour, with her propellers churning the sea to foam beneath her stern, the *Ohio* was able to move only half a mile farther.

Suddenly, with a report like a cannon shot, the towing cable parted. The battleship surged ahead and the broken towing cable whipped across her fantail with a high-pitched whistle. The other end of the cable, attached to the sub, vanished beneath the water. The decision to retain the *Alanthus's* original line now paid off. While some of the *Ohio's* deck hands reeled in the broken towing cable, others attached a marker buoy to the intact one. This would guide salvagers back to the sub. All the officers present agreed that the only way to raise the *S-Five* now would require divers and compressed air, a project beyond the scope of the ships present.

SATURDAY, SEPTEMBER 4—OFF NEW JERSEY.

The next morning the Navy ships tracked down the marker buoy. They found the *S-Five* in twenty-four fathoms. At 6:00 A.M. a ship arrived bearing a representative of the Merritt and Chapman Salvage Company. After reviewing the situation, the master wrecker advised the assembled naval officers that nothing could be done to salvage the sub at this time. At 2:30, the Navy ships steamed away, leaving the *Beaver* to keep watch over the sub until a Navy lighthouse tender could attach a more durable lighted whistling buoy.

Watching from the deck of the destroyer *Biddle*, which would take them to Philadelphia, the *S-Five's* crew could only shiver and thank their lucky stars they were no longer inside the sub. By this time most of them had recovered from the physical trauma of their thirty-seven-hour ordeal but many of them would have nightmares about it for a long time to come. On Friday, the night after the rescue, as he slept with his crewmates on a wrestling mat in the *Ohio's* gymnasium, helmsman George Bill wakened in a cold sweat. Down in the battleship's engine room, firemen had begun running water through the coal chutes and Bill had dreamed that he was back in the *S-Five's* engine room, listening to seawater slosh back and forth in the forward end of the compartment.

On Friday morning newspapers around the country broke the *S-Five's* story with front page headlines, giving readers their first dramatic, if not always accurate, description of the events off

New Jersey. "RESCUING THE CREW IMPRISONED 35 HOURS IN SUBMARINE S-5," proclaimed the *New York Times*, and "GEORGIA BOY ON SUBMERGED SUBMARINE," crowed the *Atlanta Journal.*

The headlines and the stories that went with them appeared after the rescue had taken place, but they were based on reports filed when the crew was still trapped in the sub. As a result they conveyed a sense of urgency that no longer really applied. A column in the *Boston Globe* began, "AIR BEING PUMPED TO CREW—AID ON THE WAY," and went on to describe the situation as it had existed twelve hours previously.

This lack of up-to-the-minute information guaranteed that there would be front-page headlines again on Saturday, when news of the successful rescue finally arrived. It also guaranteed that the initial reports would contain a variety of different, often wildly inaccurate versions of events, as reporters filled in the gaps in their knowledge from their own fertile imaginations.

"TELEPHONE BUOY GIVES 30 MEN ON S-5 CHANCE FOR LIVES." Declared the *New York Evening Star*, followed by:

> New York, September 3—The rescued officers and men of the United States Submarine *S-5* owe their lives to a hitherto little-tested safety device, the telephone buoy, developed during the world war. . . .
>
> When Lieut. Commander Cooke of the *S-5* realized that he was crippled . . . all he had to do was push the telephone buoy control and wait.

A column in a San Diego newspaper provided more details about the buoy's supposed role:

> TELEPHONED FROM DEPTHS: A telephone buoy tossing on the waves in the path of the steamship *General Goethals* revealed the plight of the crew of the submarine *S-5* . . . The bell on the buoy was ringing and a small boat was immediately lowered . . . The boat reached the buoy, cut in on the

telephone apparatus and then from the depths of the sea
came the message . . .

Variations on this story, including an assortment of more or less
elaborate, but all totally fictional conversations between the
*Goethals* and the submarine, appeared in newspapers from coast
to coast.

All of the "buoy stories" seem to have stemmed from a single
*Associated Press* wire story. During a telephone interview with an
AP reporter, the information officer at the New London Submarine Base described a number of rescue techniques, including the
rescue buoy. The reporter evidently didn't understand that the
officer's discussion was hypothetical. His version of the rescue
gained such wide currency that by the time the *Goethals* arrived
in Hoboken, Captain Swinson had to rebut it repeatedly. In a description of the rescue written some time later he felt obliged to
reiterate for the record, "We didn't see any buoy."

Other aspects of the story varied too. The *S-Five*'s crew ranged
from thirty to fifty-five men (and not all of them survived!). Sometimes the *Alanthus* arrived on the scene first, sometimes the
*Goethals*. One newspaper reported that the *Alanthus* was towing
the sub to port with the crew still inside her. The *Philadelphia In-
quirer* had destroyers racing to the rescue at fifty miles an hour,
far beyond the capability of ships in 1920.

Perhaps the most entertaining variation was reported in the
*New York Herald Tribune*. As the *Herald* had it, the *S-Five* sank
due to a collision with some unknown object. The sub's rescue
buoy was then discovered by the *General Goethals*, en route *from*
New York *to* Panama (reversing her actual itinerary). After de-
ploying her "war sweep cables," the *Goethals* snared the submarine and hauled her up, to the applause of "thousands of
passengers," after which the Navy ships zoomed up and released
the sub's crew using acetylene torches.

Such extravagant concoctions were unusual. Most newspapers
published fairly accurate accounts, many of them containing in-

teresting background information about naval history or biographical sketches of crewmen from the paper's home town. Several described the experience of David L. Moore, an amateur radio operator living in Farmington, Connecticut, just outside New Haven. On the evening of Thursday, September 2, Moore picked up one of the initial distress calls broadcast by the *Goethals*. He contacted a reporter for the *Boston Globe*, who in turn telephoned the Navy base at New London. Although the Navy Department in Washington knew about the *S-Five* by this time, word hadn't reached the information officer at New London, who denied knowing anything about a "sunken sub." Thus, several newspapers credited Moore with being the first to notify the Navy that one of its boats was in trouble. In fact, he may have been the first to alert the *press*.

By Saturday morning reporters had been able to question Navy sources more carefully. Some had even interviewed Captain Swinson when the *Goethals* docked in Hoboken Friday evening. As a result newspaper coverage on Saturday was more detailed and more accurate.

The *New York Times* headline for Saturday, September 4, along with its subheadings, gives a good synopsis of the accident and rescue: "WIGWAGGING SHIRT BRINGS RESCUERS TO ENTOMBED CREW—Men in *S-Five* Cut through Stern Above Water and Rigged Up a Signal—Submerged for 37 hours—Engineers of General Goethals Bore through Hull and Rescue 37 Men Safely—Air Valve Lets in Water—Floods Living Compartment and Sets Chlorine Gas Free—Men's Bravery Praised."

One of the best accounts appeared in Philadelphia's *Evening Public Ledger.* An enterprising reporter for the *Ledger* obtained permission to accompany the destroyer *Biddle,* when she left Philadelphia Friday morning. As the only news correspondent present at the scene of the rescue, he was able to interview many of participants firsthand and his impressions of Savvy and other crew members are particularly vivid. "SAILOR FORGOT TO CLOSE VALVE, OFFICER SAYS—Men Became Living Electric Wires to Drill Holes in Ship, Commander Declares—NOT A MUR-

MUR WAS HEARD DURING HOURS OF TORTURE—MORALE
CALLED PERFECT." The *Ledger's* article went on to give verbatim
much of Savvy Cooke's own description of the preceding three
days.

Articles were now accompanied by photographs. Some newspapers merely raided their photo morgues for stock reproductions of the ships involved; but others obtained stunning
photographs of the stern of the *S-Five* protruding from the sea,
often with the *Alanthus,* the *Goethals,* or the *Ohio* in the background. There were individual shots of Savvy, Captain Johnson,
and Captain Swinson, as well as group photographs of the submarine's crew. By Sunday the story had run its course. Some newspapers published follow-up articles, but these were usually on back
pages.

## SATURDAY, SEPTEMBER 4—OFF NEW JERSEY.

At 11:00 on Saturday morning, while the *Ohio* was still hovering over the sunken *S-Five*, the board of investigation reconvened
on the battleship to take testimony from the submarine's officers
and crew. Missing were four injured crewmen, who were still in
the ship's infirmary under observation, and two sailors who had
been given emergency leave to go home on one of the destroyers.
The reporter from the *Evening Public Ledger* provides a compelling description of Savvy Cooke as he appeared one day after
the rescue. The *S-Five's* commander was dressed in a borrowed
officer's uniform, because his own dress uniforms were somewhere on the ocean floor. According to the reporter, Cooke stood
up straight as he spoke, but his voice was faint, his face looked
"drawn and seamed," and his hand shook as he pointed out details
to the other officers on a diagram of the submarine.

By this time the Board's members knew the story of the sinking
and rescue, at least in its broad outlines, but it was still necessary
for them to get an account into the official record. Savvy testified
first. He didn't identify Percy Fox as the cause of the sinking in his
initial testimony, saying simply, "It was realized at this time by all

hands that the closing of the valve had not been accomplished."
When the Board asked *who* had been responsible for this crucial
step, Savvy answered that it had been Percy Fox, the chief of the
boat; but he immediately added, "that valve should be such that it
could be closed, even if water started coming through it." In doing
this, Savvy was merely continuing what he and his shipmates had
already established as their policy. If they were asked under oath
to identify the person responsible for the main induction valve,
they named Percy Fox; otherwise they said nothing. For example,
Fred Whitehead told a reporter that the accident was caused by "a
defective main air intake valve," and went on to add, "This valve
had always been hard to work." Their silence on the matter was so
uniform that only a single newspaper, the *Evening Public Ledger,*
whose reporter had been present at the site of the wreck, was able
to identify Fox as the man who caused the sinking. Most newspapers could only report, along with the *New York Times,* that the
*S-Five* had sunk due to "failure of the main air induction to work.
Who was to blame they did not know."

The board addressed other issues. They wanted to know about
the state of training of the *S-Five*'s crew, why the main induction
valve was open before an emergency dive, and how Savvy justified
omitting status reports during the dive. Their questions weren't
reproachful and they seemed to be satisfied with Savvy's answers.
After forty practice dives, he told them, his crew should have been
ready for the crash dive. In all previous dives they had performed
flawlessly. This assessment was supported by Charlie Grisham,
who testified that "the crew of the *S-Five* was as well, if not better
trained than any crew I've ever served with."

Savvy went on to state that the induction valve was open because the engines and motors used up so much air and gave off so
much heat that the engineering spaces could have become uninhabitable without the extra ventilation. He suggested that without
the main induction system, sudden closure of the conning tower
hatch or one of the bulkhead doors leading to the engine room
might have serious or even fatal consequences, due to the enormous amount of air being taken up by the diesels.

Finally Savvy noted that, in conducting the tests under "wartime conditions" without requiring reports at every step, he had merely followed the Navy's testing instructions in their literal sense. The other men who testified corroborated their commanding officer's statements and often added their own opinions in his support. For example, when the board asked Charlie Grisham if he would be willing to sail again on a submarine with the same type of ventilation system, he answered simply, "No, Sir!"

There's no question that the board found the testimony by the S-Five's crew convincing. In their final report, they concluded that the S-Five had sunk because Percy Fox had failed to close the main induction valve. They noted that Savvy Cooke had contributed to the accident by failing to examine the valve himself when he entered the control room and by not requiring reports from the crew about critical procedures during the dive. Nevertheless, they went on to observe that practice dives were supposed to be under wartime conditions and that Captain Cooke had every reason to trust his crew in general and Percy Fox in particular, as the most qualified enlisted man on the boat.

The Board concluded that an open main induction valve should *not* have been sufficient to sink the sub, if other components—like the high-pressure pump—had functioned properly. Consequently they did not recommend censure for Savvy, Percy Fox, or any other member of the crew. Instead, the Board noted that *after* the sinking the officers and crew of the sub had "conducted themselves in accordance with the best traditions of the service under exceptionally trying circumstances." In addition, it commended the officers and men of the *Alanthus* and *General Goethals* for their Herculean efforts to save the trapped submariners.

Once the Board of Investigation had concluded its work and adjourned on Saturday, the crew of the S-Five was transferred from the *Ohio* to the destroyer U.S.S. *Biddle*, bound for Philadelphia. Before they left, however, they demonstrated their respect and affection for their skipper in the most effective way possible. Savvy's friend, Captain Hart of the *Beaver*, described it in a letter:

After 37 hours of that suffering and horror, the whole crew went to Cooke yesterday [Saturday] morning and volunteered to man the *S-Five* again after she is ready for them. And I don't think there was anything grandstand about it or any idea of a bluff . . .

When the Biddle got under way for Philadelphia on Saturday afternoon, Fred Whitehead wasn't on board. On Friday Savvy had learned that the destroyer *McDougal* was leaving for New York. Summoning Fred to his cabin, he'd asked the chief, "How would you like to go to Brooklyn?" He didn't have to ask twice. Fred tells the rest of the story best. After quick approval of emergency leave, he climbed aboard the *McDougal* and "soon we were on our way to God's country. I was still sleepy, so I found an empty bunk and turned in. When I awoke, there were the lights of Coney Island and Flatbush and all of Home Sweet Home!" Best of all, there was Dorothy, waiting for him when the *McDougal* docked, healthy again and with their new son in her arms.

When the remaining *S-Five*s arrived in Philadelphia on the *Biddle* Saturday night they were welcomed at the foot of the gangplank by the commandant of the Fourth Naval District, Admiral Hughes, and by the members of the press.[11] By now the rescued submariners had recovered both physically and mentally, as their ebullient comments to the reporters demonstrated. "We have the best crew in the Navy!" boasted Seaman Second Class Joseph Yonkers, who added, "I want to be on the next dive and I want to make it with Savvy Cooke!" The following day nearly all the crew left Philadelphia, taking advantage of the leave they'd been granted to visit families and friends. Before departing they offered yet another proof of their faith in their captain by sending a

---

[11] Also waiting for them was Gunner's Mate Second Class A. B. Milliken, the only member of the *S-Five*'s crew who didn't make the voyage to Baltimore. Milliken was discharged from the hospital on the afternoon of Monday the 29th, only a few hours after the *S-Five* left port. He was waiting in Baltimore to rejoin his shipmates, when he learned about the sinking.

joint telegram to the Navy Department, renewing their desire to serve again under Savvy Cooke.

When Savvy reached Philadelphia aboard the *Ohio*, he was met by his brother Stephen, who had been granted special leave from the Naval Academy for the occasion. From Philadelphia Savvy travelled to Washington, where he made a complete report to the Navy Department, and then to the Portsmouth Navy Yard. Wherever he went the story of the miraculous escape preceded him, and he was treated with the special deference reserved for men who have cheated death. But the reception he cherished most waited for him in Fort Smith, Arkansas, where he journeyed as soon as his official duties had been fulfilled.

### NOVEMBER 1920—PHILADELPHIA NAVY YARD.

No one was surprised when Secretary Daniels ordered a formal court of inquiry into the sinking of the *S-Five*. The loss of any warship during peacetime was bound to prompt questions that only a rigorous court hearing could answer satisfactorily. Nevertheless, the hearing must have concerned Savvy. Except for a court martial, a court of inquiry is the gravest and potentially the most damaging legal proceeding that a military officer can undergo, and this would be the second such investigation Savvy had faced within six years.

From Savvy's point of view, there were significant differences between the *S-Five* and the *E-Two* episodes. Unlike the explosion on the *E-Two*, the sinking of the *S-Five* did not result in loss of life or even serious injury. As a result, to his crew and to many other people in both the Navy and the civilian world, Savvy emerged from the accident as a hero. But there was another side to the story that the Navy could not overlook. Not just any sub, but one designed to be a showpiece of the fleet, was now at the bottom of the sea. In order to prevent similar accidents in the future, the Navy had to determine the causes and, if necessary, whom to hold responsible.

The Court was convened at the Philadelphia Navy Yard on Friday, November 5, 1920. Like the court that had investigated the explosion on the *E-Two*, this one consisted of a presiding officer and two senior naval officers. Its first session was devoted largely to procedural matters, such as identifying witnesses and "interested parties" and reviewing the transcript of the Board of Investigation. Testimony began on the following Monday, but from the outset the proceedings had a different tone than the *E-Two* hearing. After the *E-Two* explosion Miller Reese Hutchison had pursued his own agenda of shifting blame for the explosion onto Savvy. In the present case there was no such third party. All of the witnesses were either members of the *S-Five*'s crew or officers who had taken part in the rescue, and these people were predisposed to take Savvy's side.

In many ways the proceedings of the court of inquiry were like a more elaborate version of the board of investigation on the *Ohio*. By the end of the second day the court had heard enough testimony to form a picture of the sinking and its aftermath. Along the way it had begun to address some of the issues that would be crucial in its final report. Why did the *S-Five* sink? Who was responsible? And how could similar accidents be prevented in the future?

Just as he had before the board of investigation, Savvy identified Percy Fox as the man who left the main induction valve open and precipitated the accident, but he followed that admission with the following remarkable statement:

I desire to say that at the time of making a crash dive there are innumerable things that must be done almost at the same instant and I can hardly hold anyone culpable, I believe, for the overlooking for an instant of one detail.

Savvy went on to point out that Fox had been distracted by other tasks immediately before the dive and reminded the Court that the *S-Five* shouldn't have sunk merely because of Fox's error. The entire crew (including Percy Fox) had taken appropriate and timely steps to save the sub, but none of these had worked. When one of the Court's members asked him, "If the induction valve had not stuck, do you believe that you would have been able to save the vessel?" Savvy answered emphatically, "Yes, I do!"

The court devoted considerable attention to the mechanical failures that had contributed to the submarine's loss, including the main induction valve, the high- and low-pressure pumps, and the Kingston valves. Although Savvy was candid in his appraisal of these flaws, he never tried to use them to shield himself. Indeed, when the court asked him if he'd willingly command such a boat again, he said he would. Not so Charlie Grisham. When the *S-Five*'s executive officer was asked, "Would you be willing or satisfied to go to a vessel of similar class with the same kind of ventilation system?" he answered emphatically, "No, Sir!"

There were numerous signs that the officers on the court were sympathetic to Savvy. One member cited the Navy's own instructions for submarines, which specifically ruled out individual reports from crewmen during crash dives. Another member volunteered the information that the high-pressure pump had failed in an H-Class submarine two years previously, just as the *S-Five*'s pump had.

Gradually the tenor of the questioning changed. Rather than challenging Savvy to justify his actions, the court began to ask his advice about how submarine design could be improved to avoid similar accidents in the future. He was happy to oblige. His suggestions included power-operated valves, sensors to register the status of hull openings, and interlocks between various components to prevent accidental flooding. Many of his remarks were incorporated in the board's final statement and several are reflected in the construction of contemporary submarines. The so-called Christmas Tree is an example: an array of indicators, mounted in the control room of every modern sub, that shows whether the sub's ports, valves, and hatches are open or closed. Such a device and the requirement for "all green" before a dive might have saved the *S-Five*. In its final report the court, like the board of investigation, held that Percy Fox was "responsible" for the sinking, but did not censure him or anyone else. Regarding the loss of the *S-Five* it stated:

> It is the opinion of this Court that the loss of the submarine S-FIVE was due to these several causes, all necessary and contributory to the final result: the initial list of the ship, failure of the main induction and torpedo compartment valves to function properly and the total disablement of the main high pressure pump. These are all material defects and show faulty design or workmanship, possibly both . . . Lieutenant Commander C. M. Cooke is exonerated from any blame . . . In failing to close the main induction valve, Chief Gunner's Mate Percy Fox, U.S. Navy, was not culpably neglectful of duty; that his attention was occupied in overcoming list of the vessel and in coaching the diving rudder men to incline vessel at proper angle.

The Court continued by commending Savvy and his men for their conduct after the sinking and to recommend that the Navy issue official expressions of gratitude to the merchant seamen who saved them. When all was said and done, the best analysis of what happened that September day may have come on the second day of testimony, when Savvy was asked, "If the valves, as you state, were unsatisfactory, was it not dangerous to attempt to dive?"

"Well," Savvy replied, "apparently it was."

ON SEPTEMBER 21, 1920, the Office of the Secretary of the Navy sent a letter to the Bureau of Supplies and Accounts, authorizing the disbursal of the following awards: Captain Johnson and Engineer Jakobsen of the *Alanthus* and Engineer Grace of the *Goethals* were to each receive gold watches, costing $300 to $400. Captain Swinson and Assistant Engineer McWilliams of the *Goethals* would receive binoculars. All the awards were to be inscribed with suitable expressions of gratitude on the Navy's behalf. A photograph of one of the award ceremonies, taken in Daniels's office, shows the secretary and Captain Earnest Johnson flanked by several other officials with the gold watch displayed on the desk in front of them. Standing there in his captain's coat, with his large hands held awkwardly at his sides, as though he isn't sure what to do with them, Johnson looks surprisingly young for a man with so many years at sea behind him.

To its credit the Navy lost no time in modifying the main induction valves in the remaining S-class boats. A memo dated September 16, two weeks after the sinking, refers to the alterations carried out in Submarines *S-Three* to *S-Nine.* When Savvy visited the Portsmouth shipyard a week after the sinking, he saw the changes being implemented in the *S-Six:* all ventilation valves were replaced with quick-closing, lever-operated models that would function even under high external water pressure. In their correspondence about the loss of the *S-Five,* the Navy's Bureau of Construction and Repair claimed that these changes had already been approved before the sinking, but there's little doubt that the events of September 1 speeded their implementation.

WHEN ASKED ABOUT THE RESCUE, the people who were involved in it responded in various ways. Eight decades later their modesty and self-effacement is particularly striking. William Grace, chief engineer of the *General Goethals,* the man who almost single-handedly cut through the hull, described his seven hours of back-breaking labor as "all in a day's work" and "no more than what others would have done." He went on to say, "I felt repaid for any trouble I had taken, when I saw the men emerge from what might have proved to be their living tomb." Instead of discussing themselves, the rescuers spoke of the men they had saved, commending their courage and fortitude. And everyone, crewmen included, joined in praising Savvy Cooke "to whose coolness, courage and capable handling of the whole affair we feel we owe our lives." The captain was, said Ramon Otto, "an inspiration to every man in the crew." The most telling tribute may have come from his friend and fellow officer, Captain Hart of the *Beaver*. "Few officers would have gone through all that Cooke did without somewhere taking some of the many wrong steps there were, simply begging to be taken—and thus very quickly ending it." For his part, Savvy took every opportunity to praise his men "for their magnificent morale, their courage, and their uncomplaining perseverance and attention to duty in those trying hours."

There was one notable exception to the general air of good feeling about the outcome of the sinking. No doubt stung by the court of inquiry's reference to "faulty design or workmanship," the Navy's Bureau of Steam Engineering issued an analysis of the accident that was marked at times by a hilariously defensive tone. In particular it devoted more than a page to Henry Love's solitary struggle to halt the flooding in the *S-Five*'s torpedo room. After some detailed calculations regarding the amount of water that could have entered the torpedo compartment and the rate of flooding, the bureau concluded that the process had taken two minutes and nineteen seconds. It then asserted that Gunner's Mate Love, while straddling a torpedo and struggling to close the valve under that icy deluge of seawater, should have calmly performed the same calculations and concluded that he should remain inside the torpedo room to battle the flooding while the door was dogged shut! If he had only done so, the *Bureau* concluded "there appears to be no reason why the boat could not have been brought to the surface without damage to the vessel or danger to the personnel."

It's unlikely that anyone else took the Bureau's remarks seriously, least of all Henry Love.

An interesting story involves the fate of the metal plate that was cut from the *S-Five*'s hull. Somehow in the midst of the rescue operations, someone thought to retrieve it and carry it aboard the

*Alanthus,* but after that it disappeared. A few weeks later, Captain Earnest Johnson was strolling down a street in Norfolk, Virginia, when, to his surprise, he saw the jagged disc on display in a shop window. The shop's owner, a Mister Shulman, revealed that the plate had been sold to him by none other than Carl Jakobsen, the *Alanthus's* chief engineer. Shulman declined to part with the memento, but after Captain Johnson wrote to the Navy Department, agents from the Justice Department persuaded him to surrender it.

The plate is now on display in the museum at the United States Navy Yard in Washington, D.C. Battered and scratched, edged by more than a hundred jagged little semicircles, the plate bears mute witness to the desperate struggle that was waged both inside and outside the *S-Five's* tiller room that day. A brass plaque affixed to its center reads:

Removed from the United States Submarine S-5 to allow the crew of that vessel to escape after being imprisoned 37 hours. The S-5, while engaged in diving exercises, flooded forward compartment and sank at 2:00 p.m., Sept. 1, 1920, in 165 feet of water. After repeated efforts the crew managed to bring the stern of the vessel to the surface, the vessel lying at an angle of 60° with the bow resting on the bottom. The crew managed to cut a small hole in the hull and by an improvised signal attracted the attention of a passing steamer, the ALANTHUS. Later the Pan-American steamer GEORGE W. GOETHALS arrived on the scene. The Chief Engineer of that vessel, Mr. W. C. Graves, assisted by the Chief Engineer of the ALANTHUS, Mr. C. Jakobsen, working with a ratchet drill and chisel, removed this plate and at 3:00 a.m., Sept. 3, 1920, the crew of the S-5, numbering 36 men, were rescued.

In a kind of nautical justice for the lives she helped to save, the *Alanthus* escaped the knacker's yard. After renovation at the Kearny Shipyard in New Jersey, the little steamer returned to the sea, where she plied the East Coast trade for a number of years.

The *General Goethals* continued sailing for the Panama Shipping Line until 1924, when she again saw brief fame. Purchased by black activist Marcus Garvey during his unsuccessful attempt to resurrect the United Negro Improvement Association, the *Goethals* was the highlight of the UNIA's 1924 convention. After that both the steamship and Garvey's plan to establish an independent African state fade from history.

OVERALL THE S-CLASS SUBMARINES were a great success. Of the fifty-one S-Boats built between 1918 and 1924, nearly all went on to serve ably through to the end of World War II. Assigned mainly to the Solomon Islands in the Pacific, they destroyed an extraordinary amount of Japanese ships, among them the heavy cruiser *Kako* and the auxiliary carrier *Shinano,* the largest warship that had ever been sunk by submarine attack. The best combat record was achieved by *S-Forty-four,* which sank three Japanese warships, including the *Kako.*

The *S-Forty-four* was also the only one of its class to be sunk by enemy action, when it inadvertently launched a surface attack on a Japanese destroyer during its fifth combat patrol. Six other S-Boats were lost due to accident. Six found their way into the British fleet and one was traded to the Polish Navy. By 1943 all S-Boats had been either withdrawn from service or assigned to secondary patrol duties.

After the war the remaining S-Boats were either scrapped or used for target practice except for a few, which had sadder histories. The *S-Fifty-one,* last submarine in the series, was rammed by the steamship *City of Rome* on the night of September 25, 1925, in Long Island Sound. With a huge hole ripped in her hull at the level of the battery room, the *S-Fifty-one* sank in less than a minute, taking all but three of her thirty-six crewmen with her.

An eerily similar fate awaited the *S-Five*'s sister ship. On December 15, 1927, the *S-Four* was conducting submerged speed runs off the coast of Massachusetts when she was accidentally run down by a Coast Guard cutter. The collision tore open the sub's hull and flooded her battery room. Within seconds she was on her way to the bottom in 108 feet of water with six crewmen trapped in the forward torpedo room and the remaining thirty-four isolated in the stern. Because both battery room and control room were flooded, it was impossible for them to raise the sub. Divers located the wreck within hours and even communicated with the six men in the torpedo room by means of tapping on the hull, but severe weather conditions delayed salvage operations until all forty men had died.

Sad though it was, the loss of the *S-Four* had a number of salutary consequences, including new navigational regulations to restrict surface vessels from areas where submarines were operating and the institution of a 25 percent hazardous-duty bonus for submariners, putting them on a par with naval aviators. In addition, the tragedy was a primary motivation for Lieutenant Charles Momsen's pioneering work in submarine rescue techniques.

IN LATE OCTOBER of 1920—exactly thirty days after the sinking—the U.S.S. *Mallard* was dispatched to salvage the *S-Five*. Finding the wreck wasn't difficult, thanks to the marker buoy that had been set up, but the salvage operation was unsuccessful. A series of Atlantic gales hampered the work. By November 19 the weather had deteriorated so badly that the effort was postponed until the following spring. On May 3 the Navy's salvage ship U.S.S. *Falcon* arrived at the site and divers set to work dynamiting the sub's internal bulkheads and sealing points of leakage with quick-setting concrete.

Interestingly, the divers found that the starboard bow rudder was rigged out and set at hard rise, while the port rudder had been broken off short, consistent with Captain Hart's speculation about the difficulty the *Ohio* had in starting to tow. In addition, divers found evidence to support some of the sub-mariners' recollections. In the control room they found that the cover had been removed from a spare lubricating oil tank. And when they opened the battery room hatch from the outside, they encountered a mass of material that had jammed up under it, including a piece of sixteen-gauge metal that had been virtually molded to the underside of the hatch. Their impression was that the entire battery room deck had been blown upward by a powerful explosion, probably the one heard by the *S-Fives* Wednesday night.

In spite of all their valiant effort, Navy divers were unable to raise the sub. On August 29, 1921, the Navy officially called off the salvage attempt and struck the *S-Five* from the list of ships. It's understandable that the Navy would willingly invest thousands of dollars and hundreds of man-hours on attempts to salvage the *S-Five*. If she had been brought to the surface, the damage she had suffered during the accident and salvage could have been repaired. In his testimony before the board of inquiry, Savvy estimated that it would take about half a million dollars ($4.5 million in today's currency) to make the sub operational again.

In all, Navy divers made 477 separate dives on the *S-Five*. They were hampered by poor visibility, strong ocean currents, and the fact that the hull could not be made watertight. The head diver on the salvage team believed that this was due to structural damage from a powerful explosion in the battery compartment. Considering the difficult and dangerous conditions under which they worked, it was a tribute to the Navy divers that none of them was injured. Diving on the wreck proved to be so challenging that the Navy's Director of Salvage Operations, Commander C. W. Fisher, recommended that the wreck be used as an official training site. In another of the historical links that make this story so interesting, nineteen years later the *Falcon* was the dive ship from which "Swede" Momsen rescued the crew of the *Squalus*.

MOST OF THE CREWMEN from the *S-Five* remained together after the rescue, but the Navy didn't grant their request to serve under Savvy Cooke again. Instead they were assigned to Submarine *S-Nine*. In July, 1921, they participated in what was then the longest cruise on record for American submarines, sailing from Portsmouth, New Hampshire, via the Panama Canal and Hawaii, to the Philippine Islands.

William Grace, the chief engineer of the *Goethals*, served on the old steamship until she was sold in 1924, after which he became the port engineer for Panama Lines in the city of New York. He retired from that post in 1970.

Carl Jakobsen, the chief engineer of the *Alanthus*, joined the Standard Oil Company and began working on the big ships of the Esso fleet. Years later, when he was chief engineer of the tanker *C. A. Canfield*, he ran into one of the men he had helped to rescue. Quartermaster George Bill, the sailor who'd been at the helm when the *S-Five* made her last dive, was serving as second mate on the *R. P. Resor*, another Esso tanker. His reunion with Jakobsen was extensively reported in the fleet's official bulletin, along with a detailed account of the sinking and rescue.

John Longstaff fulfilled Savvy Cooke's high expectation. He remained in the submarine service and during the last two years of World War II commanded a submarine wolf pack against the Japanese in the Pacific. Operating out of the Marshall Islands, his Submarine Squadron Fourteen was one of the Navy's premier attack groups. In 1970 Longstaff retired from the Navy with the rank of captain and settled down in a small town in Connecticut. By an odd twist of fate, in 1939 he acted as a Navy spokesperson during the *Squalus* rescue.

After leaving the *Alanthus*, Captain Earnest Johnson commanded a succession of small vessels before retiring to his native island of Saba, where he began to write his autobiography. The only copy in existence, which was published by his son in mimeographed form, ends with the rescue of the *S-Five*. Captain Johnson was buried near his house on Saba in a small cemetery over-looking the sea.

TRAGEDY CONTINUED TO STALK Savvy Cooke. Less than a year after the escape from the *S-Five* in the spring of 1921, his beloved older daughter, Temple, fell ill and died. She was only six years old. The event may have severed the family's last ties to Fort Smith. In June 1922, Savvy's parents, along with Anne and Savvy's sister Cornelia, set sail for the west coast on the hospital ship *Mercy*. They were moving to San Pedro, California, where Savvy had purchased a house for them.

In spite of the heartbreak, Savvy's career advanced steadily. In November 1920 the Navy ordered him to sea as the executive officer of the U.S.S. *Rainbow*, the flagship for the Twelfth Submarine Flotilla. A year later he took command of the flotilla, when it was stationed in Hawaii. In 1923, he spent ten months in the Philippines, after which he began a succession of increasingly important administrative positions in the Navy Department with occasional forays back to sea. For two years he was commandant at the Mare Island Naval Station on the west coast. Next came a "blue water" tour lasting from October 1925 until April 1928, when he served as gunnery officer on the U.S.S. *Idaho*.

Savvy's next tour at sea extended from April 1931 until June 1933, when he was commander of Submarine Division 11. After brief stints as commandant of the Naval Station at Guantánamo Bay in Cuba and in the office of the Chief of Naval Operations in Washington, he became logistics officer on the staff of the commander in chief of the U.S. Fleet. Once again he was back at sea, this time on the fleet's flagship, the U.S.S. *Pennsylvania*. After another two and a half years in the office of the CNO, he returned to the *Pennsylvania* as its commanding officer in February 1941. He was still in command of the battleship ten months later on December 7, 1941, when Japanese airplanes swept out of the Hawaiian sky.

Savvy was fifty-five years old in 1941 and had attained the rank of captain. A photograph taken on the deck of the *"Pennsy"* shows a thin, erect officer in formal white. The face beneath the brim of the cap has aged, but he's lost none of its sternness, and the eyes have the same quiet shrewdness that characterized them through-out his life. He had married again in 1921 to Mary Louise Cooper MacMillan, whom he met when she was a reporter for a Honolulu newspaper. His old friend Chester Nimitz served as best man at the wedding. With Mary he had three children: Maynard (born 1925 in Vallejo), Charlotte (born 1930 in Washington), and at last a son, Charles Maynard Cooke III (born 1931 in Honolulu). Mary and the children usually traveled with him to his postings around the world, but in 1941 they remained in California in the house that Savvy had built for them in Sonoma. He left them there de-liberately when he was sent back to Hawaii, because the war with Japan that he'd predicted for years seemed imminent. It wasn't the first time that history proved him right, nor the last, but it was surely the most dramatic vindication.

On the morning of December 7 Savvy had just finished break-fast on board the *Pennsylvania,* when the first Japanese bombs went off. He hurried up to the bridge and remained there during the rest of the attack, calmly directing the defense of his ship. At one point, he walked across the quarterdeck to inspect the dam-age done to the forward guns by a bomb. Noticing that a Japanese machine gun bullet had lodged in the teakwood deck, he asked his marine orderly for a pocket knife. Ignoring the Japanese planes, which continued to strafe the battleship, he dug the bullet out "for a keepsake."

In all the *Pennsylvania* had sixty-seven casualties, including twenty-nine men killed and thirty-eight wounded, but the ship herself was only slightly damaged. It was a stroke of luck. The Jap-anese had specifically targeted the flagship for destruction; but the *Pennsylvania* had been moved into drydock for repairs shortly before the attack. The *Utah,* which had taken her place along "battleship row," was sunk instead.

Mary and the children heard about the attack on the radio and for some time were unsure whether Savvy was alive or dead. The news that he'd survived came with more good tidings. The *Pennsylvania* was coming home. Several weeks after the attack, she sailed for San Francisco, arriving there on December 29. After repairs and training exercises, the battleship rejoined the war in August, but Savvy had been transferred back to Washington to join the Navy's Strategic Planning Division. In 1942 he was promoted to rear admiral, and by 1945 he had become the head of Strategic Planning. In belated recognition of his contributions, after the war he was awarded the Distinguished Service Medal.

Although most of Savvy's time was spent in Washington, he saw his share of action too. While advisor to the allied forces, he participated in the Normandy invasion. At noon on D-Day, during the height of the German defensive barrage, he went ashore with General Thomas Handy to assess the progress of the landing. After a stroll up and down the beach, during which his helmet was struck by shrapnel from an exploding ammunition cache, he returned to the flagship with the recommendation that the pinned-down soldiers could use more senior officers on the beach!

During the Pacific campaign Savvy was one of the principal advocates of the transition from battleships to aircraft carriers that transformed the Pacific Fleet. At the conclusion of the war he served as advisor to Fleet Admiral King during the meetings between allied heads of state at Casablanca, Quebec, Teheran, Cairo, Malta, Yalta, and Potsdam.

Because of his behind-the-scenes role, history books usually don't do Savvy Cooke justice. He would probably have been an outstanding fleet commander, but those who were in a position to know believed that he performed far more valuable service in Strategic Planning back in Washington. As one of his former Annapolis classmates put it, of all those unsung heroes who helped win the war, "his name stands at the top."

After the war, Savvy spent two years in China, where he tried unsuccessfully to bolster support for the Chinese Nationalists. His final days at sea came between 1947 and 1948, when he served as commander of the Pacific Fleet. In May 1948, he retired from the Navy and moved into the stone farmhouse he'd built with his own hands in Sonoma County. He died in 1970 and is buried near his brothers in Arlington National Cemetery.

# Epilogue: The *S-Five*

AFTER 1921 the *S-Five* disappeared and for many years remained lost in the great anonymous graveyard of the Atlantic. In 1989, 1990, and 1991 she was relocated by civilian sport divers. Today she lies about forty-eight miles southeast of Cape May, New Jersey, on a flat, sandy bottom in 160 feet of water. At this depth the wreck remains accessible only to expert recreational divers, but every year several dozen still visit her.

The *S-Five* rests with her bow pointing northeast and her hull listing twenty degrees to the port side. Surprisingly, she's remarkably intact. Most of the external damage to her hull has been caused by the Navy's salvage teams and by civilian souvenir hunters. From a distance the long veils of fishing nets that trail from her periscopes give her a wraithlike appearance. In places her wooden decking has fallen away, exposing the steel framework that supported it. Running along her spindle-shaped hull beneath the decking is a long cylinder, the eighteen-inch pipe of the main induction system. It's bent halfway through its length, angling out from the hull like the harpoon of some larger-than-life Ahab.

Up close the hull is covered with marine growth—tiny, multicolored fans of sea anemones flickering constantly in and out, with occasional bright metallic scars where divers have chipped away the encrustations to get at souvenirs. Inside the sub a fine layer of silt covers everything and forms a layer several inches thick on the deck. The anemones aren't as numerous here. Half-familiar shapes loom everywhere, weirdly distorted by the silt and overgrowth: pipes, valves, levers, and the bright gleam of glass dials, still intact.

In the stern the tiller room door remains tightly closed, just as Savvy Cooke left it, but the other watertight doors have been blown off their hinges by the salvage divers and lie scattered across the deck. The forward end of the battery room is covered by a tangled mass of debris that obscures the torpedo room door, remnants of the flood that tumbled into the bow when the *S-Five* stood on her nose.

At the stern the twin propellers and their matching rudders are visible, flanked by the extended diving planes, and just aft of these on the starboard side a dark jagged hole. Roughly circular and as wide as a man's shoulders, it looks much as it did eighty years ago, when forty men crawled through it to safety.

Overall the *S-Five* seems remote and peaceful, free of the ghosts that haunt other wrecks. The crew of the *S-Five* went on to write their stories in other times and places, leaving her to continue her journey alone. Someday a great storm may move her out into deep water or she may crumble into the sea floor, but until that day she remains a wordless reminder of a fascinating and heroic episode in naval history.

# Appendix A

# NAUTICAL LEXICON

AFT: toward the rear of a ship.

AIR MANIFOLD: an array of valves and gauges in the control room that regulates and directs the high-pressure air supply in the submarine.

AIR VENT: a vent in the top of a ballast tank that allows air to escape so that the tank can fill with seawater.

BALLAST TANKS: large tanks (usually) located outside a submarine's pressure hull, used to control the sub's buoyancy by filling with varying amounts of seawater.

BILGE: a space inside the hull, but beneath the deck, containing machinery and other components that don't require easy access and acting as a sump for water and oil.

"BOSUN": short for "boatswain," a petty officer in charge of rigging, sails, anchors, and other deck activities.

BREAST DRILL: a hand drill configured like a manual egg beater, with a padded end and a side-mounted hand crank.

BULKHEAD: a partition between compartments, usually reinforced and watertight.

CHIEF PETTY OFFICER: a senior enlisted rating, assigned to leadership positions. (See Appendix B.)

CONNING TOWER: a flattened cylindrical tower extending above a submarine's deck containing the steering platform, periscopes, and bridge.

CRASH DIVE: an emergency dive, usually performed during wartime, when a submarine is either under attack or preparing to attack another ship.

DIVING RUDDER: an adjustable horizontal plane on either side of the hull, usually at both bow and stern, which directs the sub's motion either up or down.

ENSIGN: the lowest rank for naval officers, except for Midshipman. (See Appendix B.)

FATHOM: a nautical measure of depth: one fathom equals six feet.

FORWARD: toward the front end of a ship.

HEAD: shipboard restroom, derived from the days of sail, when crewmen retired to the cutout seats in the rigging beneath the bowsprit (that is, in the "head" of the ship).

HEAVE TO: nautical term for bringing a vessel to a halt.

HELM: general term for a ship's steering mechanism.

KINGSTON VALVE: valve located in the bottom of a ballast tank to let in seawater.

KNOT: nautical unit of speed. One knot equals one nautical mile (6,080 feet) per hour, or a little more than one and one-sixteenth statute mile per hour.

LEAD-ACID CELL: single component of the electrical storage battery used in submarines and automobiles.

MAIN INDUCTION VALVE: a large valve used to ventilate the interior of a submarine.

"OLD MAN": slang term for a device used to insert torpedoes into their launching tubes.

PORT: left, or the left side of a ship.

RATCHET DRILL: a hand drill with an internal ratchet that converts forward pressure into rotation.

STARBOARD: right, or the right side of a ship.

STERN: the aft end of a ship.

TORPEDO: a motorized underwater missile, either guided or un-
guided.

WINDLASS: a cylindrical turnstile, used to pull in cables and anchor chains.

# Appendix B

# RATINGS AND RANKS
# IN THE NAVY

ENLISTED RATINGS BEGIN at Seaman Recruit and go up to
Master Chief. There is a conceptual jump between Petty Officer
and *Chief* Petty Officer. While Petty Officers are technicians,
Chief Petty Officers are managers and have different uniforms.

> Seaman Recruit
> Seaman Apprentice
> Seaman
> Petty Officer Third Class
>            Second Class
>            First Class
> Chief Petty Officer
> Senior Chief
> Master Chief

Officers are classified as either line (seagoing) or staff (largely
bureaucratic).

> Midshipman (Cadets at the Naval Academy in Annapolis)
> Ensign

Lieutenant Junior Grade
Lieutenant
Lieutenant Commander
Commander
Captain
Rear Admiral
Vice Admiral
Admiral
Fleet Admiral

# Afterword: Author's Note

I CHOSE TO WRITE *Under Pressure* in an informal narrative style in order to make it more accessible for the general reader. In other words, so it would be more fun to read. There's no extensive bibliography and there aren't many footnotes. (The ones I've included are also for fun.)

But this choice raises questions about accuracy. Without detailed references, how is the reader to know which events in the book are real and which originated in the author's imagination to fill in gaps in the historical record? How much, if any, of the dialogue represents what was actually said? And are *any* of the thoughts and emotions to be trusted?

These questions become especially relevant in the case of the *S-Five*, since virtually no records survived the sinking. Savvy and his shipmates barely escaped with the clothes on their backs (and sometimes not even those). So, how do I know what went on, what was said, what was thought?

In writing this book I owe my understanding of events to three primary resources: the official records of the Navy's board of investigation, the subsequent court of inquiry, and a remark-

able set of documents contained in the Hoover Archives at Stan-
ford University in Palo Alto, California. These consist of personal
recollections set down by members of the *S-Five's* crew in the
days and weeks following the rescue. Apparently some of these
accounts were dictated to a Navy yeoman on the battleship
*Ohio* on the day after the rescue, but others were addressed to
Cooke at later times, judging from the dates included in their salu-
tations.

Whatever the circumstances of their composition, twenty of
these first-hand accounts found their way into Cooke's personal
papers, which are preserved in the Hoover Archives. Taken together they form an extraordinarily vivid picture of what it was
like for these men during and after the sinking.

Newspaper articles about the sinking can be obtained from li-
braries and newspaper morgues around the country, but I can't
recommend them as sources of information. Most of the stories
are inaccurate to some degree, many of them wildly so. The photographs that accompany them are much better, but regrettably
these are preserved as microfilm records, which don't lend themselves to accurate reproduction. Consequently they're not included here. (They're well worth the effort for those who care to
look them up.)

Even with the available resources, details of the accident are
not always clear. Like the newspaper accounts, the personal recollections are filled with inconsistencies and even some outright
contradictions regarding what happened, to whom, and when.
Many are vague about what happened in the final hours before
the rescue, not surprising considering what these sailors under-
went. One of the most difficult challenges in writing this book was
sorting through the different versions to find the thread of truth
(or at least agreement) among them.

So, how much of what you've just read was true and how much
did I make up?

*All* of the *events*, both large and small, actually happened. In
addition, I took great pains to establish an accurate chronology.

However, the precise clock times that precede various sections are in most cases merely my best estimates, based upon the handful of times that were actually reported and a careful analysis of the intervening events. I included them to help the reader keep track of what was going on simultaneously in different places during the sinking.

Regarding statements and thoughts that I attribute to people in the story, I based all of them explicitly, if not verbatim, on material in the personal recollections or in court testimony. The only exceptions are a few trivial bits of dialogue. For example, I don't know whether Cooke actually yelled, "Dive! Dive!" to initiate the crash dive. He may have used different words, but he clearly ordered it in some way, and I felt justified in manufacturing a plausible version.

In the interest of clarity I decided to limit the number of individuals I would follow in the narrative. With first-hand recollections from more than two dozen people and direct references to nearly a dozen more, the cast of named characters dodging in and out of the story would otherwise have become unwieldy and confusing. However, I did not make up characters, combine individuals, or ascribe thoughts or actions of one character to another. As a result, I was obliged to ignore several rather engaging personalities and to exclude a number of fascinating, if isolated, incidents, but I felt that was a fair price to pay for a truthful account. To fill in the missing pieces, the interested reader is encouraged to obtain the personal accounts in their entirety. Reproductions can be ordered (for a nominal fee) from the Hoover Archives (Tel: 650-723-3563; Ref: Cooke Collection, Box 25.)

LEST ANYONE THINK that I overcame the difficulties in writing this book by myself, I would like to thank some of the many people who helped me along the way. These include:

Dr. Robert Love, Professor of History at the United States Naval Academy in Annapolis, Maryland, who steered me west.

Russell McKechnie of McLean, Virginia, who reviewed the manuscript for technical accuracy, and Julie Taub, who helped with its final preparation.

Arthur Wells, at DolArt Publishing in Chico, California, who tracked down several useful biographical anecdotes.

Aparna Mukherjee and her colleagues at the Hoover Archives on War, Revolution and Peace in Palo Alto, California, who put up with my idiosyncrasies for two full days.

The staffs at the New London Submarine Museum and Library in Groton, Connecticut; the National Photographic Archives at College Park, Maryland; and the Naval Historical Foundation, the National Archives, and the Library of Congress, all in Washington, D.C.

AS FOR WRITING THE BOOK, I'd have been lost without the many talented and generous people who read and reread draft after draft, patiently correcting my infelicities and suggesting better ways of doing things. These include my long-suffering family (especially my mother, Betty, and my brother, Chris, who were always ready to critique at short notice); my agent, Albert Zuckerman; and Bill Rosen and Andrea Au at The Free Press, without whose patient guidance this book would never have seen print. Last, but certainly not least, I wish to thank Charles M. Cooke III and Maynard Horiuchi, whose cooperation, understanding, and support made it possible to tell their father's story at last.

# Index